A CONTRASTIVE TRANSFORMATIONAL GRAMMAR

Arabic and English

Dr. Muhammad Ali Alkhuli

Publisher
DAR ALFALAH
P.O. Box 818
Swalieh 11910
Jordan
Tel & Fax 009626-5411547

A CONTRASTIVE
TRANSFORMATIONAL GRAMMAR

Arabic and English

Dr. Muhammad Ali Alkhuli

Publisher

DAR ALFALAH
P.O. Box 818
Swalieh 11910
Jordan
Tel & Fax 009626-5411547

TABLE OF CONTENTS

---

[1] For phonemic symbols, see Appendix I.

PREFACE

Transformational theory is one of the recent descriptions of language. It has been originally applied to English by different linguists, whose transformational descriptions of that language have taken several forms.

What the author intends to do here is to apply this transformational theory to Arabic, which has not entered seriously till now into the field of modern linguistic research. Arabic has always been described as it was done one thousand years ago.

This new attempt in this book moves Arabic into the realm of modern linguistics. It is also a step towards grammar universality since at the deep-structure level almost the same rules account for both Arabic and English. Further, it is a contribution to contrastive analysis, as it contrasts English and Arabic at another linguistic level and locates areas of similarity and areas of difference.

The author hopes that this research may be useful to specialists interested in Arabic grammar, English grammar, transformational theory, universal grammar, applied linguistics, and contrastive linguistics.

MUHAMMAD ALI AL-KHULI

CHAPTER ONE

INTRODUCTION

I.1   *The Purpose*

The purpose of this study is to design a new grammatical description
of Arabic and then to compare Arabic to English through this new
description, which is based on a modern linguistic theory, i.e., the
transformational theory.

The variety of Arabic that is under consideration is Modern Standard
Arabic. There are different reasons of selecting this variety. Firstly,
Standard Arabic is the variety known all through the Arab World and
most probably outside the Arab World whereas other colloquial
varieties are known basically as local dialects. Secondly, Standard
Arabic is more systematic and better controlled than the colloquial
dialects of Arabic, which makes Standard Arabic a more convenient
subject of scientific analysis and contrast.

It must be known that the designed grammar is just a sample one.
It mainly deals with the most common patterns of Arabic and this is
secured through choosing a representative sample of grammatical
structures.

In brief, this study aims at devising a transformational grammar for
Arabic then finding out where Arabic and English are different and
where they are similar. This study also aims at testing the degree of
universality of a certain deep structure in order to see how far that
structure can account for languages other than English.

1.2   *The Advantage*

The advantage of using the same grammatical model for Arabic as
is used for English is that it reveals what is common to both languages
("universal") and what is different ("particular"). This result can be
beneficially employed in teaching English to the native speakers of
Arabic and teaching Arabic to the native speakers of English.

I.3   *The Procedure*

The procedure used in this study involves the following steps: 1) collecting a representative sample of Arabic sentences, i.e., a corpus, 2) choosing the model of the transformational-generative grammar which seems to work best for Arabic, 3) postulating the appropriate deep structure for each sentence, 4) writing a set of branching rules to generate each sentence, 5) writing transformational rules to map the "deep structures" onto the "surface structures", 6) collapsing the separate rules into a scheme which will constitute a fragment of the grammar of Arabic.

I.4.   *Content*

This work rests upon a particular theory which is illustrated in Chapter II. In this chapter, there will be a discussion of the need for a theory, the definitions of a transformational grammar and a generative grammar, the reasons for using such a grammar, the phrase-structure (PS) rules, lexicon, the transformational (T) rules, the morphophonemic rules, and the evaluation criteria.

The third chapter will present the corpus phonemically transcribe and translated into English. It will also contain a section that proves the high representativeness of the used sample.

The fourth chapter presents the chosen base and the reasons why this model and not another was chosen, defines the constituents of the base, and describes the corpus according to the new model.

The fifth chapter presents the lexicon with its syntactic and semantic features.

The sixth chapter, which is the most important part of the work, devises the T-rules that operate on the PS-rules of Chapter IV. In this chapter, there will be some hints of comparison between Arabic and English. However, such a comparison is not the main purpose of this work; it is so lengthy that it would need a separate book.

The seventh chapter tests the efficiency of the grammar by trying to apply the transformational rules of Arabic to produce Arabic surface structures.

The eighth chapter suggests some applications of this work and some follow-up studies.

1.5.   *Complexity*

This type of grammar may seem overly complicated. However, this complexity is not inherent in the grammar but is due mostly to certain external factors.

The first factor is the recent growth of the transformational theory. It first appeared in 1957 with the publication of Noam Chomsky's *Syntactic Structures*, was revised by Chomsky in 1965[1] and has since developed in several different directions. The most recent developments have not been incorporated in this book, which was begun over a year ago.

The second factor is the relative strangeness of the theory and its formalization. People are accustomed to traditional grammars or to immediate constituent (IC) theory. The algebraic form of the T-generative approach baffles many readers. More familiarity with the form will change the negative attitude towards it to a positive one.

The third factor stems from the attempt of the TG grammarians to be as explicit as possible. The explicitness irritates readers who are used to making intuitive leaps when reading a grammar of their own language.

The fourth factor is the nature of the language itself, which is generally a complicated system. A true description of such a system is necessarily intricate.[2]

---

[1] Noam Chomsky, *Aspects of the Theory of Syntax* (Cambridge: The M.I.T. Press, 1965).

[2] H.A. Gleason, *Linguistics and English Grammar* (New York: Holt, Rinehart and Winston, Inc., 1965), pp. 296-298.

CHAPTER TWO

THE UNDERLYING TRANSFORMAITONAL THEORY

II.1.   *The Need for a Theory*

The major aim of a comprehensive linguistic analysis is to separate all the grammatical sequences in the language under investigation from the ungrammatical sequence and to reveal the structure of the grammatical ones. This analysis should depend upon a clear and well-defined theory. This dependence is necessary to give the analysis the minimal requirements of systematic methodology, clear purpose, and well-defined terminology.   As a result, the theory will render the analysis devoid of inner-contradictions and confusion with other linguistic approaches or analyses.   The theory, therefore, gives the analysis its philosophy, justification, terminology, and, in brief, its own identity.

II.2.   *A Definition of Transformational Grammar*

There has been a lot of controversy about what is to be considered a transformational or nontransformational grammar.   Nevertheless, one can adopt the view that "any grammar that assigns to each sentence it generates both a deep structure and a surface structure analysis and systematically relates the two analyses is a transformational grammar (whether it uses the label or not)"[1]

The statement of the relationship between the two structures, i.e., the deep structure and the surface structure, is called "a transformation". This relation is treated as though it were a process and stated in the form of a rule applicable to the input deep structure to product the output surface structure".[2]   The deep structure gives the meaning of the sentence.   It is an abstract "structure that one assumes on the basis of

_____

[1] John Lyons, *Introduction to Theoretical Linguistics* (Cambridge: University Press, 1968), p 248.

[2] H.A. Gleason, *An Introduction to Descriptive Linguistics* (New York: Holt, Rinehart and Winston, Inc., 1955), pp. 172.

the meaning of a sentence and its syntax. A surface structure is closer to physical reality in that it concretely specifies the syntactic structure necessary for spoken or written communications".[3]

However, it has always been an important issue to decide how much of the structural description is to be placed in the deep structure and how much in the surface structure. This question accounts for the existence of a variety of T-models for the same language presented by several linguists. It also accounts for the linguists' continual modification of his own model.

The T-grammar usually has four types of rules. The first type is the phrase-structure (PS) rules, which are supposed to be highly regular or, more properly, explicate the syntactic regularities of the language. The second type is the lexical (L) rules, where the irregularities of the language appear. The third type is the T-rules, which take care of what cannot be done or can only be done clumsily in Ps-rules. The fourth type is the morphophonemic (M) rules, which assign phonemic shapes to the morphemes.[4] To generate a sentence, one has to run through PS-rules, L-rules, T-rules, and then M-Rules respectively.

II.3.   *Generative Grammar and its Relation to the T-grammar*

A generative grammar is a system of rules which explicitly describes the structure of the sentences of the language it accounts for. This explicitness of description is the main characteristic and advantage of such a grammar.

However, the term "generation does not mean the physical production of sentences. It is the identification of a sequence of words as a sentence in the language".[5] To put it differently, each sequence of words that conform to the rules of the grammar is a sentence; otherwise, it is not.

So, very simply, a generative grammar is the explicit one, which runs on step by step in a computer like manner leaving nothing to the reader's intelligence. But this does not mean that a generative grammar is necessarily transformational.[6] A grammar may be generative, but

---

[3] R. A. Jacobs and P.S. Resenbaum, *English Transformational Grammar* (Waltham: Blaisdell Publishing Company, 1968), p.21.

[4] Examples of PS-rules, and T-rules appear in Chapters IV, V, VI respectively.

[5] H. A. Gleason, *Linguistics and English Grammar*, p. 247.

[6] John Lyons, *Introduction to Theoretical Linguistics*, p. 155.

non-transformational. In this case, there will be a rather long set of branching rules with detailed categorical and functional symbols.[7] Such a nontransformational generative grammar is certainly complicated and lacks simplicity because it does not take advantage of assuming a deep structure and a surface structure of each sentence.

On the other hand, every T-grammar is generative.[8] There has been no T-grammar which is not generative at the same time, since all T-grammars, especially the Chomskian ones, describe the sentences of the language in an explicit and clearly-defined manner.[9]

II.4   *Reasons for Using the T-theory*

There are several reasons for preferring the T-theory to other types of grammars such as the traditional grammars of the IC (immediate-constituents) grammar:

a) The T-grammar does not look at the sentence as simply made up of various constituents. It views it as derived from another underlying structure through a transformation process.[10] This view is more informative about the nature of the language.[11]

b) The T-grammar accounts for the speaker's ability to produce and understand an indefinite number of new sentences",[12] sentences that he hears or produce for the first time.

c) It takes into consideration the difference between the competence and the performance of the native speaker. It focuses on the intrinsic competence and not on the actual performance, unlike the descriptive grammar. In other words, the T-grammar is a mentalistic theory concerned with the mental reality that underlies actual linguistic behaviour.[13]

---

[7] Branching rules are rules that divide or sub-classify elements. For examples, see section II.5.5.

[8] A T-grammar is generative by accident and not by definition.

[9] The terms, T-grammar and generative grammar, are, after all, a matter of convention: different writers give them different definitions.

[10] Robert B. Lees, "Transformation Grammars and the Fries Framework", in Harold B. Allen (ed.), *Readings in Applied English Linguistics* (New York: Appleton-Century-Crofts, 1964), p. 142.

[11] Examples are in Chapter IV.

[12] *Ibid.*, p. 176

[13] Noam Chomsky, *Aspects of the Theory of Syntax* (Cambridge: The M.I.T. Press, 1965), p.4.

d) The T-grammar aspects the view that the "linguistic theory is concerned primarily with an ideal speaker-listener, in a completely homogenous speech community, who knows its language perfectly and is unaffected by such grammatically irrelevant conditions such as memory limitations, distractions, shifts of attention and interest, and errors in applying his knowledge of the language in actual performance".[14]

e) The T-grammar is purely linguistic since it deals with competence whereas the data of the descriptive or empirical grammar are socio-physco-linguistic since they deal mainly with actual performance.

f) It accounts efficiently for complex sentences that are accounted for clumsily by other grammars.

g) It accounts for the native speaker's ability to see the semantic synonymity of two or more sentences which have different surface structures.[15]

h) It also accounts for his ability to see the semantic difference between two or more sentences though they have similar surface structures.[16]

i) It accounts for his ability to understand a sentence though some of its main parts are deleted.[17]

j) It explicitly accounts for an ambiguous structure,[18] i.e., a structure that has two different semantic interpretations.[19]

k) It accounts for the native speaker's ability to distinguish between grammatical and ungrammatical sentences in an infinite set of structures.

These characteristics of the T-grammar will be elaborated in the coming sections of this chapter and in the actual application of the theory in the following chapters.

However, this does not mean that other grammars, i.e., nontransformational ones, do not account for any of the previously-mentioned matters. What is meant is that the T-grammar accounts in a more

---

[14] *Ibid*, p. 3.

[15] e.g., The boy ate the apple
The apple was eaten by the boy.

[16] e.g., Ali promised John to behave himself.
Ali asked John to behave himself.

[17] e.g., (You) come here.

[18] Wallace L. Chave, *Meaning and the Structure of Language* (Chicago: The University of Chicago Press, 1970), p. 63.

[19] e.g., Flying planes can be dangerous.

efficient, systematic, and explicit way. It does it in a mathematical way: the given, the process, and the result. This parallels the grammatical input, transformation, and the output respectively. Both mathematics and the T-grammar rest on a theory, stick to a procedure, and employ a system of conventional notation, i.e., symbols.

II.5.   *Phrase-Structure Rules (PS-rules)*

11.5.1 *Introduction*

The phrase structure or the base (the deep structure) is one part of the syntactic component;[20] the other part is the T-rules, which determine the surface structure. However, the exact nature of the base is still undetermined; different transformationalists propose different hypotheses about it. The most interesting ones will be those that push the base towards what might be called "universal or philosophical grammar", a grammar that approaches neutrality and avoids bias to a certain language.

Each base consists of a system of rules that generate a highly restricted set of basic or terminal strings, each with a structural description called a "base phrase-marker".

II.5.2   *The base Universality*

A lot of modern grammarians are interested in seeking for a universal syntactic base, a base common to most languages, if not all. The under-lying assumption of such a base is the existence of a "human language".[21] the argument for this assumption is that language ex-presses essentially meanings, ideas, and emotions, the great part of which is universal. Therefore, the deep structures of languages should contain universal elements, which reveal those universal meanings.

There is another argument for the base universality. Every individual possess an innate human faculty of language; every normal child develops his own skill of speech and comprehension. He also constructs a partial grammar given a sample data of his native language. This

---

[20] The other components of language are the semantic component and the phonological component.

[21] Chomsky, *op. cit..*, p. 117

innate linguistic faculty common to all humans necessitates a minimal number of base elements common to all languages.

A third argument may be found in translation. The fact that a language can be translated into any other language indicates that there is a lot of semantic and syntactic commonality among all languages.

Naturally, different bases vary in the degrees of the universality they show. However, the roader the elements of the base and the more semantic they are, the more universal the base is.

To archive this universality, the features of a language are to be reduced to universal properties of language. One may think of the deep structure consisting of layers, the deepest of which is the most universal. It is for this most universal that some researchers direct their efforts.

II.5.3 *The Sentence in PS-rules*

Although there have been various descriptions of the base, the sentence, which is conventionally represented by #S#, has always appeared as the initial symbol in the base, with its two boundary symbols.

This S is different from the sentence in traditional grammar, which gives the sentence a definition[22] that can indicate anything from a single word to a volume. S here is "a designation for a unit which is basic to grammatical patterns as described by a transformational grammar".[23] It is what the grammar itself defines and covers.

Instead of trying to define S before writing the grammar, the grammar itself is the definition of all and only the grammatical sentences in the language. In other words, the grammar tells you what a sentence is – if the grammar produces it, it is a sentence.

II.5.4 *The Types of PS-rules*

The S in the previous section divides or "branches" into other constituents, each of which may branch into other sub-constituents. This branching continues till the last rule that shows on the right hand of the arrow "terminal symbols", which allow no further branching.

Such branching should be kept to a minimum to reduce the com-

---

[22] The traditional definition is that a sentence is a group of words that give a complete meaning. A word may give a complete meaning, so may a long story.

[23] H. A. Gleason, *An Introduction to Descriptive Linguistics*, p. 190.

plexity of the grammar and achieve more generality of the rules within the language and more universality of the base. In addition, these branching rules are given different labels by different tranforma- tionalists, such as PS-rules, base rules, deep-structure rules, constituent- structure rules, or IC rules.

What are the types of PS-rules? To answer this question, it is more convenient to use an exemplary set of rules that belong to no language:

(1)   # A #

(2) $A \rightarrow \begin{Bmatrix} B \\ c \end{Bmatrix} + i$

(3)   B → D + (e)
(4)   D → F + g / - X
(5)   F → h + (A)

The first rules gives the starting point or the initial symbol surrounded by two boundary symbols. The second rule rewrites A as B or c and adds i. Such a rule is called "alternative", because it includes two alternatives marked by braces. The third rule rewrites B as D or D + e. The parentheses around e indicate "option". The fourth rule is conditioned by the presence of the environment X, which makes the rule "context-sensitive".[24] The fifth rule rewrites F as h + (A), where A appears on the right of the arrow in this rule and on the left of the arrow in the second rule. This recurrence of A in the fifth rule makes the rule "recursive".

Such recursiveness is necessary to reduce the complexity of the grammar and increase its power and adequacy. Once the fifth rule is applied, it is required to repeat the application of all the previous rules beginning with the second. This process of re-application may continue infinitely with the effect of producing and endless variety of sequences or sentences. However, the recursiveness is an optional process since A is within parentheses.[25]

In addition, the PS-rules must take a certain order in the process of constructing or using them. It is wrong to apply the fourth rule, for example, before the third. The reason is that every symbol on the left of the arrow in a certain rule must appear on the right of the arrow

---

[24] Late T-grammars are in disfavour with such rules to avoid unnecessary complexity in the base. However, such restrictions are placed in lexicon and structural descriptions.

[25] Recursiveness has to be optional because embedding is optional: not all sentences include embedded sentences.

in a previous rule. In other words, the input of a rule must be a part of the output of a previous rule.

To sum up, the PS-rules may be alternative or non-alternative, context-free or context-sensitive, recursive or non-recursive, but they are necessarily ordered.

On the other hand, the PS-rules cannot delete (Rule 6), and (Rule 7), or rearrange (Rule 8) because these functions are performed by T-rules. The PS-rules, however, may replace (Rule 9) or expand (Rule 10):[26]

(6) $M \rightarrow \emptyset$

(7) $N \rightarrow N + O$

(8) $P + Q \rightarrow Q + P$

(9) $X \rightarrow \begin{Bmatrix} Y \\ Z \end{Bmatrix}$

(10) $S \rightarrow T + W + V$

II.5.5   *Further Terminology in PS-rules*[27]

There are two types of symbols in the PS-rules. The first type is the "terminal" symbols, which cannot be branched out or expanded any more such as c, e, g, and h in the first five rules mentioned in the previous section, II.5.4. The second type is the "non-terminal" symbols, which allow further branching-out such as A, B, D, and F in the same five rules.[28]

The sequence of terminal symbols that is produced through the PS-rules is called a "terminal string" or a "kernel string". However, this string is not to be confused with a "kernel sentence"; the difference between the two is clear. A kernel string is the output of PS-rules without the application of any T-rules, whereas a kernel sentence is generated from a kernel string to which obligatory T-rules are applied without applying any optional T-rule.

A terminal string consists of several "substrings"; each substring may be one element or more. The string can be represented by a "phrase-marker" through a labelled bracketing or a tree-diagram with labelled nodes. Each node dominates all the nodes branching down from it.

---

[26] Emmon Bach, *An Introduction to Transformational Grammars* (New York: Holt, Rinehart, and Winston, Inc., 1864), pp. 36-41.

[27] Andreas Koutsoudas, *Writing Transformation Grammars* (New York: McGraw-Hill Book Co., 1966), pp. 1-14.

[28] Terminal symbols are conventionally written in small letters and non-terminal symbols in capital letters.

Looking back again at the first five rules in Section II.5.4., one may see that h + c + i + g + e + i is one possible terminal string. The phrase-marker of this string may be represented in the following tree-diagram:

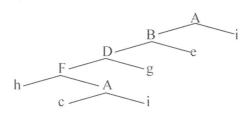

In this diagram, A dominates B and i; B dominates D and e; D dominates F and g, and so on. Each symbol has a "derivational path". The path of h, for example, is (A, B, D, F, h); the path of g is (A, B, D, g). No line in any path in the diagram of the phrase-marker is allowed to cross another.

II.6.   *The lexicon*

So far, the PS-rules have been discussed. By applying these rules, the meaning of a sentence is partly determined. However, the determination of meaning is not completed unless one applies the lexical (L) rules.

Such application involves the selection of the proper lexical entries to substitute for the terminal symbols of the terminal string, which is the PS-output. If the selection is proper, the sentence is well-formed, i.e., grammatical. But if the selection is not proper, the sentence will be less grammatical though not ungrammatical; in this case, it often has a metaphorical interpretation.

This leads to the term "degrees of grammaticality".[29] "The bird flew" is certainly more grammatical than "the heart flew". The first sentence obeys the selectional rules strictly: "+fly" is a feature of "bird" and a "+bird" is a feature of "fly". On the other hand, the second sentence does not obey the selectional rules: "+heart" is not a feature

---

[29] Noam Chomsky, *Aspects of the Theory of Syntax*, p 77.

of "fly", nor is "+fly" a feature of "heart"; the two words "heart" and "fly" are concatenated against the rules of lexical selection.

The lexicon contains the information required by phonological, semantic, and syntactic components of the grammar. It thus informs of the irregularities of the language,[30] leaving the regularities to appear in the PS-rules and T-rules. Most of this information is given in the form of positive +, negative -, or positive-negative ± features.

II.7.   *Transformational Rules*

II.7.1   *The Nature of T-rules*

II.7.1.1   *Introduction*

The T-rules are applied after applying the PS-rules and choosing the suitable lexical entries. That is why they are called "supplementary rules" as well; their application is subsequent to the application of PS-rules and L-rules. Therefore, they contrast with the PS-rules, which are called "elementary rules" in the sense that they receive initial application.

II.7.1.2   *The Function of T-rules*

"One major function of the T-rules is to convert an abstract deep structure that expresses the content of a sentence into a fairly concrete surface structure that indicates its form".[31]

Such a function may be performed in a variety of processes, the number and the nature of which are still far from being agreed upon by transformationalists. Bach, for example, sees the processes as follows.[32]

(1)	deletion	: $a + b \Rightarrow \emptyset + b$
(2)	replacement	: $a \Rightarrow b$
(3)	expansion	: $a \Rightarrow b + c$
(4)	reduction	: $a + b \Rightarrow c$
(5)	addition	: $a \Rightarrow a + b$
(6)	permutation	: $a + b \Rightarrow b + a$

---

[30] *Ibid.*, p. 88.

[31] *Ibid.*, p. 136.

[32] Emmon Bach, *An Introduction to Transformational Grammars*.

On the other hand, Fillmore uses other T-processes, which are partly different.[33]

(1)	deletion	$: a + b \Rightarrow a + \emptyset$
(2)	permutation	$: a + b \Rightarrow b + a$
(3)	copying	$: a + b \Rightarrow b + a + b$
(4)	fronting	$: a + b + c \Rightarrow b + a + c$

In spite of these differences in the function of T-rules, the view welcomed by most T-grammarians is that a T-rule cannot introduce meaning-bearing elements, which are supposed to be introduced by PS-rules and L-rules.

II.7.1.3   *The Condition of T-rules*
The T-rule is applied under a condition, which is "structural analysability".[34]   This means that a T-rule applies only to a string analysable in terms of elements provided by the deep structure. In other words, there should be a structural description of the string and this SD should be analysable in terms of PS-symbols. This condition is necessary to prevent the T-rules from applying indiscriminately to any string. It is thus an essential control on the "machine" of the grammar.

II.7.1.4   *The Order of T-rules*
The T-rules must be constructed and applied in a certain order for the reasons of both simplicity and grammaticality. It is not economical to repeat the necessary T-rules after each transformation. Further, the lack of order may produce ungrammatical sentences. For example, singular T-rules should be applied to a constituent sentence before it is embedded in a matrix sentence[35] and to a matrix sentence after embedding a constituent sentence.[36]   Otherwise, the resulting sequence will be ungrammatical, which defeats the whole purpose of the grammar, i.e., generating grammatical sequences.[37]

---

[33] Charles Fillmore, "A Proposal Concerning English Prepositions", in F.P. Dinneen (ed.), *Monograph Series on Language and Linguistics*, No. 19 (Washington, D.C.: Georgetown University Press, 1966), pp. 19-31.
[34] John Lyons, *Introduction to Theoretical Linguistics*, P. 259.
[35] These terms are defined in the next section.
[36] Noam Chomsky, *Aspects of Theory of Syntax*, p. 135.
[37] e.g., Subject-verb concord should be applied to the adjective clause before embedding it: the trees which are watered grow better.

II.7.2   *The Types of T-rules*

The T-rules can be classified into two types: "optional" and "obligatory". The obligatory rules have to be applied to a kernel string to produce a kernel sentence, to which other optional rules may be applied to produce a variety of other sentences.

In addition, the T-rules may be subdivided into two other types in terms of the base. The first type operates on one base whether optionally or obligatorily; it is called "singular" or "single-base" transformation. The second type operates optionally on two or more terminal strings; it is called a "generalized" or "double-base" trans-formation. A generalized T-rule either embeds a constituent sentence in a matrix or conjoins tow sentences or more without making any of them subordinate to the others. However, this type of T-rule, i.e., the generalized one, is disfavoured now. It has been done without by introducing into the base optional recursive rules.

II.8.   *Morphophonemic Rules (M-rules)*

After the application of PS-rules, L-rules, and T-rules, one applies the M-rules. They, in fact, operate on the output of T-rules and assign to each morpheme its proper allomorph.[38] This assignment is con-ditioned by phonetic or morphemic environments. However, such rules are generally excluded from this study to control the scope of the work.

II.9.   *The Criteria for Evaluating*
a T-Grammar

Of the four types of rules, the most difficult ones to construct are the PS-rules and T-rules. It is in these parts of grammar that most differences occur. But the T-theory assigns for itself the criteria for evaluating competing grammars. These criteria are:

a) Adequacy: this is tested by determining if the generated sequences are acceptable as grammatical to a native speaker.[39] If all the sequences generated by a grammar are grammatical, then the grammar passes the test of adequacy; otherwise, it does not.

---

[38] e.g.,   ring + past → rang

   talk + past → talked

   put + past → put

[39] Noam Chomsky, *Syntactic Structures* (The Hague: Mouton and Co., 1957), p. 49.

b) Formality: a grammar is formal if it offers a consistent theory of language, with its own system of evaluation. A grammar that meets the formality criterion is certainly closer to science than a grammar that fails to do so.

c) Explicitness: a grammar is explicit if it does not rely on the reader's intelligence in its description of the language. An explicit grammar tells about the conditions under which every rule may be applied, the type of the rule, the option or the obligation of its application, the order if there is any, and the context-sensitivity if necessary. In brief, all significant information is explicitly expressed somewhere in the grammar.

This explicitness quality is borrowed from science, which is always explicit in its theories, rules, and applications. *A grammar is, or in fact should be, a scientific theory of a language*; therefore, it should be as explicit as typical sciences. The more explicit a grammar is, the more scientific it will be.

d) Generality: a grammar is general if it rests on a general theory, i.e., a theory independent of any particular language.[40] On the other hand, a grammar that rests on a theory of a particular language deprives itself of universality, a major characteristic of science. This generality will make a grammar abler to reveal the facts of language because it will make use of insights in other languages, which will throw more light on the language under investigation.

e) Simplicity: this evaluation measure of alternative grammars implies the following elements:

1. minimizing the number of symbols in the grammar,
2. minimizing the number of rules,
3. over-all simplicity: simplifying a part of a grammar must not complicate other parts. On the contrary, it must lead to their simplification as well,[41]
4. making the rules readable by avoiding unreasonable lengths or too many conditions of application,
5. making a rule as powerful as possible by avoiding over-classification,
6. avoiding ad hoc rules, which are divised to solve a particular problem for the time being without taking the over-all simplicity into consideration.

---

[40] Noam Chomsky, *Syntactic Structures*, p. 50
[41] *Ibid*, p. 55.

II.10. *Further Remarks on the T-theory*

In addition to all that has been mentioned about the T-theory (its rules, definitions, evaluation, etc.), there are some important points that are mention-worthy.

a) The T-grammar is not a pedagogical grammar. It is a purely linguistic one, which is not meant to be taught to beginners learning a foreign language.

b) The T-grammar is not superior to non-transformational grammars for all purposes. It might be that its superiority is restricted to certain purposes whereas the traditional grammar, for example, is preferred for other purposes.[42]

c) The T-grammar is not a model for a speaker or a hearer.[43] It is merely a statement of relations between structures. A speaker does not construct his sentences by running through PS-rules, L-rules, T-rules, and then M-rules. Nor does a hearer understand these sentences by processing them that way.

d) There is no one T-grammar of a certain language because a grammar is a hypothesis and with a lot of grammarians working on language X, one expects a lot of hypotheses accounting for the same data. Similarly, there may be more than one traditional grammar and more than one structural grammar for a certain language.

e) There is not a mechanical discovery procedure in the T-theory. The researcher makes use of a variety of activities: intuition, guessing, past experience, and some methodological hints.[44] The rules undergo several revisions and are subject to continual modification and even cancellation. The researcher cannot devise a rule and leave it un-touchable. The rule has to continue to be under test while devising all the other rules of the grammar.

---

[42] H. A. Gleason, *Linguistics and English Grammar*, p. 297.
[43] Noam Chomsky, *Aspects of the Theory of Syntax*, p. 9.
[44] Noam Chomsky, *Syntactic Structures*, p. 56.

CHAPTER THREE

THE CORPUS

III.1. *Introduction*

This chapter presents the corpus for which the grammar accounts and to which the T-theory is to be applied. Further, this chapter deals with the method used to choose this particular corpus, i.e., the sampling method.

III.2 *Method of Sampling*

The method that suits this study is the method of stratified sampling. The population or the universe, i.e., the language under consideration, is divided into strata.[1] Then each stratum is given the chance of appearing in the sample at least once.

This stratified sampling need not be proportional here for two reasons. Firstly, the frequency of each stratum is not known and, in fact, it is difficult to know it because the language, or an language, is an infinite number of sentences and, therefore, it is not a limited population; more than that, it is continuously being created. Secondly, even if the frequencies of strata are known, they are not needed here since this research does not include, nor does it need to, any statistical operations or formulae. It is a research of grammatical relations, not a research of figures and statistical predictions.

The method of stratified sampling is more suitable to the purpose than random sampling. Random selection means giving every individual, i.e., member in the population, an equal chance of being selected and giving every sample of a certain size an equal chance as well, say, by drawing a paper and replacing it with another on which a sentence is written. Such randomness does not necessarily supply a representative

---

[1] "Strata" here is a statistical term which simply means classes or types. It has nothing to do with "grammatical strata". Further, these strata are provided by grammar books of Arabic, as shown in Bibliography. However, the sentences themselves are not taken from any source.

sample. It may happen that a randomly-selected sample includes a narrow section of the language especially because a sample, by definition, is of a limited size.[2]

For similar reasons other methods of sampling have not been used. Systematic sampling, which is choosing every individual with a certain rank and its multiples such as the fifth, tenth, fifteenth, may neglect individuals with special importance. So may cluster sampling, which divides the population into clusters, randomly chooses some clusters than randomly chooses some individuals from the chosen clusters.[3]

To sum up, the method of sampling that has been found convenient for the case and the purpose is stratified sampling. Other methods such as random sampling, systematic sampling, and cluster sampling have been shown to be unsuitable here because they imply the probability of producing a weakly representative sample.

III.3. *The Representativeness of the Sample*

As has been shown in the previous section, the sampling method that will be employed is the stratified method. The strata to which the population is divided are the following: sentence types, verb types, noun types, object types, particle types, and miscellaneous types. More details about these types appear in the coming sections.

However, this classification is done in traditional grammatical terms and not in the T-theory terms for these reasons. Firstly, using traditional classification will serve as an external evaluative criterion of the sample representativeness. Secondly, this study has not reached the T-application yet. Thirdly, and as a result, traditional classification of Arabic is the only thing available at this early stage of work. Fourthly, describing the sample according to the T-theory is the job of all the coming chapters.

III.3.1 *Types of Sentences*

The sample, i.e., the corpus, is made to include the following sentence types:

---

[2] Helen M. Walker, *Elementary Statistical Methods* (New York: Henry Hold and Company, 1949), pp. 265-268.

[3] George J. Mouly, *The Science of Educational Research* (New York: American Book Company, 1963), pp. 178-190.

a)	Statement:	$1, 2, 3, 4, 5^4$
b)	Interrogative sentence:	45^5
c)	Imperative sentence:	51
d)	Request sentence:	48
e)	Verbal sentence:	3, 4, 5, 11, 12
f)	Nominal sentence:	25, 35, 39
g)	Affirmative sentence:	46, 47, 50
h)	Negative sentence:	20, 26
i)	Conditional sentence:	52
j)	Embedded sentence:	18, 27, 46, 50
k)	Relative sentence:	46
l)	Modifying sentence:	50

III.3.2 *Types of verbs*
    Besides including a variety of sentence types, the corpus is made to include a variety of verbal types:

a) Present verb:
        1.   Indicative: yakburu $(6)^6$
        2.   Subjunctive: ?aktuba (27)
        3.   3. Jussive: yaktub (28)
b) Past Verb: 2, 3, 4, 5^7
c) Transitive Verb:
        1.   With one object: 42
        2.   With two objects: 2
d) Intransitive Verb: 3, 19, 24
e) Active Verb: 4, 5,^{7}
f) Passive Verb: 29
g) Exclamatory *?af9al*:   39

III.3.3 *Types of Nouns*
    The sample is also made to include a wide variety of nouns:

---

[4] These numbers refers to the numbers of the sentences in the corpus of Section II.4. These sentences are just examples of the type; there may be others that are statements as well.
   [5] These types do not exclude each other: a verbal sentence may be affirmative or negative, a statement or a question.
   [6] Phonemic symbols are in Appendix I.
   [7] All terms in Section III.3 are traditional terms. A verb is present or past according to form, not meaning because a verb present in form may be past in meaning, e.g., *lam yaktub ?al walad* "The boy did not write".

a) Doer:[8]   ?al waladu (2)
b) Sub-doer: ?al risa:latu (29)
c) Active participle: ka:tibun (34)
d) Passive participle: maktu:batun (35)
e) Exaggerative form: Daħu:kun (7)
f) Likened quality: jami:lan (21)
g) Abstract noun: ?iħtira:man (23)
h) Possessive construct: kita:batu ?al waladi (41)
i) Demonstrative noun: ha:ða (10)
j) Proper noun: sami:run (23)
k) Common (generic) noun: walada (31)
l) Masculine noun: waladu (43)
m) Feminine noun:
        1. by form: kita:batu (41)
        2. by usage: na:ra (38)
        3. by signification: layla: (20)
n) Singular noun: ħablu (3)
o) Dual noun: waladayni (30)
p) Plural noun: ?awla:du (40)
q) Inflected noun:
        1. nominative case: kita:bu (1)
        2. accusative case: ?iħtira:man (23)
        3. genitive case: mu9allimi (23)
r) Uninflected: huna (47)
s) Pronouns:
        1. separable pronouns: huwa (25)
        2. inseparable pronouns: ta (46)
        3. separation pronouns: huwa (25)

III.3.4 *Types of Objects*

The sample is made to include a variety of object types as well:

a) Direct object: ħablan (5)
b) Indirect object: samiran (2)
c) Cognate (absolute) object: mašyan (33)
d) Purpose object: ?iħtira:man (23)
e) Adverbial object of place: huna: (47)

---

[8] "Doer" refers to the surface *fa9il*, which is not necessarily the actual agent.

f)   Adverbial object of time: ?amsi (44)
g)   Accompaniment object: ?al nahra (22)

III.3.5 *Types of Particles*

Further, the sample is made to include a variety of particles:

a)   Negator: ma: (20)
b)   Interrogator: ?a (49)
c)   Jussive governor: lam (28)
d)   Subjunctive governor: ?an (27)
e)   Conjunction: wa (49)
f)   Preposition:
          1.   separable preposition: fi: (31)
          2.   inseparable preposition: bi (13)

III.3.6. *Miscellaneous Types*

The sample is also made to include a lot of other different types:

a)   Theme and rheme (*mubtada? and xabar*):   1, 6, 7, 17, 18
b)   ka:na and its sisters: 9, 21
c)   ?inna and its sisters: 30
d)   ka:da and its sisters: 32
e)   Genus-negator *la:* :   31
f)   Comparative *?af9al*:   ?aTwal (39)
g)   State (manner):   da:hikan (24)
h)   Subordinates (*twa:bi9*):
          1.   Adjective:
                    a.   derived: ?ahmar (42)
                    b.   underived: ?allaði: (46)
          2.   Emphasis: nafsuhu (43)
          3.   Appositive: sami:run (44)
i)   Vocative: sami:ru (37)
j)   Temptation: ?al bayta (37)
k)   Warning: ?al na:ra (38)
l)   Exception: sami:ran (40)

After choosing the proper sampling method, i.e., stratified sampling, and setting the strata, the corpus is made to include all the types of sentences, nouns, verbs, particles and other types which appear in the strata.

Through this procedure, the representativeness of the corpus is established.   But this does not mean that the corpus is completely representative; it only means that it is most probably highly so. In addition, the corpus does not need to be completely representative because the purpose is to devise a "sample" grammar not a "complete" grammar, and because even with this limited corpus one has more than enough problems to deal with.

In fact, the corpus is deliberately meant to include the important and frequent patterns of Arabic and to exclude rate, insignificant, or old patterns such as *?ixtiSa:S, ?ištiga:l, tana:zu9, ?istiga:θa, nudba, tarxi:m*, and *?ism ?al fi9l*.

III.4.   *The Sentences of the Corpus*

Each sentence in this corpus is phonemically transcribed to make it readable to those who do not know the Arabic alphabet. Further, each sentence is followed by its equivalent meaning in English to make it understood by those who do not know Arabic. For the same purpose, the corpus is made to include the minimal number of vocabulary items. In addition, each sentence is given a number, which will be frequently referred to.

1.   ?al kita:bu 9ala ?al Ta:wilati[9]
      = The book is on the table.
2.   ?a9Ta: ?al waladu sami:ran kita:ban
      = The boy gave Sameer a book.
3.   ?inqaTa9a ?al ħablu
      = The rope separated (or broke)
4.   fataħa ?al mifta:ħu ?al ba:ba
      = The key opened the door.
5.   qata9a sami:run ħablan
      = Sameer cut a rope.
6.   ?al waladu yakburu
      = The boy is growing.
7.   ?al waladu Daħu:kun
      = The boy laughs too much.

---

[9] The words in these sequences are transcribed as they appear in the lexicon, i.e., without morphophonemic changes. However, they have their case endings.

To find the meaning of an Arabic word, one may consult Appendix IV, the Glossary.

A perfect phonemic transcription should present suprasegmental phonemes as well: stresses, pitches, and junctures. However, for the purposes of this work, it suffices to have the segmentals only.

8.   kataba sami:run
       = Sameer has written.
9.   ka:na sami:run huna:
       = Sameer was here.
10.   maša: ha:ða ?al waladu
       = this boy walked.
11.   maša: ha:ða
       = This walked.
12.   ra?a: ?al waldu nafsahu
       = the boy saw himself.
13.   kataba ?al waladu bi ?al qalami
       = The boy wrote with the pen.
14.   ?al waladu kataba bi ?al qalami
       = The boy wrote with the pen
15.   bi ?al qalami kataba ?al waladu
       = The boy wrote with the pen.
16.   9ala ?al Ta:wilati kita:bun
       = There is a book on the table.
17.   busta:nu ?al bayti kabi:run
       = The garden of the house is large
18.   ?al baytu busta:nuhu kabi:run
       = The house has a large garden.
19.   maša:
       = He walked.
20.   ma: mašat layla:
       = Laila did not walk.
21.   ka:na ?a; baytu ǰami:lan
       = The house was beautiful.
22.   sa:ra sami:run wa ?al nahra
       = Sameer walked along the river.
23.   waqafa sami:run ?iħtira:man li ?al mu9allimi
       = Sameer stood up in respect of the teacher.
24.   waqafa sami:run Da:ħikan
       = Sameer stood up while laughing.
25.   9umaru huwa ?al 9a:dilu
       = Omar is the just one.
26.   la: ?aħada fi ?al bayti
       = There is nobody at the house.
27.   ?uri:du ?an ?aktuba risa:latan
       = I want to write a letter.

28. lam yaktub ?al waladu
    = The boy did not write.
29. kutibat ?al risa:latu
    = The letter was written.
30. ?inna ?al waladayni wasi:ma:ni
    = The two boys are really handsome.
31. la: walada fi: ?al bayti
    = There is no boy at the house.
32. ka:da ?al waladu yamši:
    = The boy was about to walk.
33. maša: mašyan
    = He walked well.
34. ?inna sami:ran ka:tibun darsahu
    = Sameer will surely write his lesson.
35. ?al risa:latu maktu:batun
    = The letter is written.
36. ma: ?ajala ?al bayta
    = How beautiful the house is!
37. ?al bayta ya: sami:ru
    = Stick to the house, Sameer.
38. ?iyya:ka wa ?al na:ra
    = Beware of the fire.
39. sami:run ?aTwalu min layala:
    = Sameer is taller than Laila.
40. kataba ?al ?awa:ldu ?illa: sami:ran
    = the boys except Sameer wrote.
41. kita:batu ?al waladi ĵami:latun
    = The boy's handwriting is beautiful.
42. fataħa ?al mifta:ħu ?al ba:ba ?al ?aħmara
    = The key opened the red door.
43. maša: ?al waladu sami:run ?amsi
    = The boy himself walked.
44. maša: ?al waladu sami:run ?amsi
    = The boy, Sameer, walked yesterday.
45. ma: ?ismuka
    = What is your name?
46. ?inqaTa9a ?al ħablu ?allaði: ?ištara:ta hu
    = The rope which you bought has been cut.
47. maša: sami:run wa 9aliyyun huna:
    = Sameer and Ali walked here.

48.   ?ala: tusa:9iduni:
        = Will you please help me.
49.   ?a maša: ?al waladu
        = Did the boy walk?
50.   ha:ða waladun sa:fara ?abu:hu
        = The boy's father has travelled
51.   ?uktub ?al darsa
        = Write the lesson.
52.   ?in tadrus tanǰah
        = If you study, you will pass.

CHAPTER FOUR

PHRASE-STRUCTURE RULES[1]
(PS-RULES)

IV.1.   *Introduction*

In the previous chapter, a representative sample of Arabic sentences has been submitted and the method of sampling has been introduced and justified.   In this chapter, a PS-model will be chosen, modified, justified, and applied to these sentences.   These PS-rules are merely immediate-constituent rules that are applied to the base only, i.e., the deep structure.

IV.2.   *The Chosen PS-model*

The model that has been chosen is Fillmor's,[2] which was devised originally for English:

PS1:   S → (Mod) Aux Prop
      where   S   = sentence
               Mod   = modality
               Aux   = auxiliary
               Prop   = proposition
               the arrow → = is rewritten
               the parentheses ( ) = optionally included.

PS2:   Mod → $\begin{cases} \text{SentenceAdverbial} \\ \text{Time Adverbials} \\ \text{Interrogative} \\ \text{NegaitveElements} \end{cases}$

The braces indicates free choice within them.
Sentence adverbials are those that modify all the sentence rather than a particular word in it such as "therefore" = liha:ða.

---

[1] This is often referred to as PS-rules.
[2] Charles Fillmore, "A Proposal Concerning English Prepositions", *Monograph Series on Language and Linguistics*, No. 19, pp. 19-23.

PS3:   Prop → V (Erg) (Dat) (Loc) (Inst) (Ag)
       where   V   = verb
               Erg   = ergative[3]
               Dat   = dative; the indirect object
               Loc   = locative; the place referent
               Inst   = the instrument of the action
               Ag   = the actual doer of the action

$$\text{PS4:} \quad \begin{bmatrix} \text{Erg} \\ \text{Dat} \\ \text{Loc} \\ \text{Inst} \\ \text{Ag} \end{bmatrix} \rightarrow \text{NP}$$

       where NP = nominal phrase

PS5:   NP → P (Det) (S) N
       where   P   = preposition
               Det   = determiner
               S   = sentence
               N   = noun

IV.3. *The modification of Fillmore's Model*

It has been found that Fillmore's model needs two modifications to account more adequately for Arabic sentences. The first modification changes V in PS3 into VI, which means "verbal", a term that covers typical verbs and adjectives. The original V in Fillmore's PS3 cannot cover adjectives. The coming chapters and especially Chapter VI and VII will show how adjectives fit in this VI slot. The second modification is to put S in PS5 after N instead of being before it because in Arabic the embedded S that modifies N comes after N; the modification simplifies the T-rules
   So PS5 → P (Det) N (S)

---

[3] Ergative is the subject of an intransitive verb and the object of a transitive verb, e.g.,
   He moved *the stone.*
   The stone moved.
The ergative is thus the NP that is most attached to V. It is what Fillmore symbolized later as Obj in "The Case for Case" in Emmon Bach and Robert T. Harms (eds.), *Universals in Linguistic Theory* (London: Holt, Rinehart and Winston, 1968), p. 24.

IV.4.   *The Justification for Choosing*
Fillmore's Model

The question that may arise is why Fillmore's model and not another has been chosen as a base for Arabic. In other words, is there anything special about this model that makes it more suitable to account for this Arabic corpus? The following sections will try to answer this question.

IV.4.1 *Chomsky's Model*[4]

Before evaluating Chomsky's model, one may look at its rules:

PS1:   S → NP Predicate-Phrase
PS2:   Predicate-Phrase → Aux VP (Place) (Time)

$$
\text{PS3:}\quad VP \rightarrow \left[\begin{array}{l} \text{Copula Predicate} \\ V \begin{cases} \text{NP (Prep - Phrase)(Prep - Phrase)(Manner)} \\ \text{S} \\ \text{Predicate} \end{cases} \end{array} \right]
$$

$$
\text{PS4:}\quad \text{Predicate} \rightarrow \begin{cases} \text{Adjective} \\ \text{(lik) Predicate - Nominal} \end{cases}
$$

PS5:   Prep-Phrase → Direction Duration, Place, Freqence, etc.
PS6:   V → CS
PS7:   NP → (Det) N (S)
PS8:   N → CS[5]

where   S   = sentence
        Aux   = auxiliary
        NP   = nominal phrase
        VP   = verbal phrase
        N   = noun
        CS   = complex symbol

This model of Chomsky is not the suitable one here for the following reasons:

1. It is obvious that its first rule sits English but does not suit Arabic, because Arabic sentences usually begin with a verb and not with a noun.

---

[4] Noam Chomsky, *Aspects of the Theory of Syntax*, p. 106.
[5] There is no need to continue with his other selectional rules.

2. This model emphasizes the notations of subject and predicate as necessary for semantic interpretation although these notations are surface ones and should not belong to the deep structure. Consider these examples:

The key opened the door.

The door opened.

The janitor opened the door with the key.[6]

Looking at these sentences, one does not find any constant semantically relevant function shared by the subjects of these sentences. Although the key, the door, and the janitor are subjects, they are an instrument, an ergative, and an agent respectively.

3. Chomsky unnecessarily differentiates between the nominal phrase and the prepositional phrase when Fillmore successfully shows that all nominal phrases are prepositional phrases in the deep structure.

Therefore, Chomsky's model does not suit Arabic, and uses misleading notions that do not suit English or Arabic deep structure.

IV.4.2 *Other Chomskian Modified Models*

There are other models that follow the example of Chomsky such as Gleason's[7] and Roberts's.[8] In addition to the criticisms against Chomsky, one may criticize these two models for the following reasons:

1. They are over-classified bases. Gleason classifies his verb into seven types and his noun into ten types. Roberts classifies his verb into five types. This over-classification decreases the base generality, universality, and simplicity.

2. With that over-classification, the two models of Gleason and Roberts and made English-biased, i.e., suitable to English only because Arabic does not have the same kind or number of noun or verb classes as English.

3. The two models do not suit Arabic right from the initial rule which both have: S → NP + VP. This rule does not fit in with Arabic where the verb usually precedes the noun.

---

[6] Charles Fillmore, "A Proposal Concerning English Prepositions", *Monograph Series on Language and Linguistics*, No. 19, p. 21.

[7] H. A. Gleason, *Linguistics and English Grammar*, p. 251.

[8] Paul Roberts, *English Syntax* (New York: Harcourt, Brace and World, Inc., 1964), pp. 1-88.

4. This over-classification implies the problem of cross-calssific-cation: a verb that is classified to be intransitive may be transitive as well such as "melt"; a noun classified as singular may be used as plural such as "class".

IV.4.3. *The Advantages of Fillmore's Model*
Comparing Fillmore's model to Chomsky's and others' models, one can see that:

1. The elements of Prop in PS3 in Fillmore's model are put in free order; T-rules will order these elements in the manner that suits Arabic or English.

2. Fillmore's base has no over-classification, which makes it the simplest and most general of all: it has the fewest number of symbols and rules. It has five rules while the others range between eight and eighteen; it has eighteen symbols while the others range between twenty-three and seventy-two. By being non-over-classified, Fillmore's model avoids being English-biased, cross-classified, and complicated.

3. It avoids the surface notions of subject and predicate and emphasizes the underlying functions of NP as agent, ergative, instrument, locative, and dative. These functions are very much semantical, which pushes the model closer to universal or human language. In fact, the universality was in Fillmore's mind when he designed his base: "In their deep structure, the propositional nucleus of sentences in all languages consists of a V and one or more NP's, each having a separate case relationship to the P (and hence to the V)".[9]

In brief, Fillmore's base is simpler, more efficient, and more universal that other competing models. In addition, it can be a common base to both English and Arabic.

IV.5. *Describing the Corpus according to Fillmore's Model*

In the previous section, the argument has been that Fillmore's model suits Arabic better than other models. This section will present a description of the corpus according to Fillmore's base, i.e., appealing only to the elements mentioned in the base. The description will

---

[9] Charles Fillmore, "The Case of the Case", in Emmon Bach and Robert T. Harms (eds.), *Universals in Linguistic Theory*, p. 51

act as a further test of the base suitability to Arabic. Further, such description is certainly tentative because no sentence in the corpus can be described or accounted for through the PS-rule only: every sentence is the output of several transformations. Therefore, a through description[10] cannot be made except when T-rules are available.

1. ?al kita:bu + 9ala ?al Ta:wilati
   Erg   +   Loc[11]
2. ?inqaTa9a + ?al waladu + sami:ran + kata:ban
   Aux Vl +   Ag   + Dat   + Erg
3. ?inqaTa9a + ?al ~~j~~hablu
   Aux Vl   + Erg
4. fata~~ha~~ + ?al mifta:~~h~~u + ?al ba:ba
   Aux Vl +   Inst   + Erg
5. qta9a   + sami:run + ~~h~~ablan
   Aux Vl +   Ag   + Erg
6. ?al waldu + yakburu
        Erg   + Aux Vl
7. ?al waladu + Da~~h~~u:kun
   Ag   + Aux Vl[12]
8. kataba + sami:run
   Aux Vl + Ag
9. ka:na + sami:run + huna:
   Aux   + Erg   + Loc
10. maša + haða + ?al walad[13]
    Aux Vl + Ag$_1$ +   Ag$_1$
11. maša   + haða
    Aux Vl + Ag
12. ra?a: + ?al waladu + nafsahu
    Aux Vl +   Ag   + Erg
13. kataba + ?al waladu + bi ?al qalami
    Aux Vl +   Ag   + Inst
14. ?al waladu + kataba + bi ?al qalami
        Ag   + Aux Vl +   Inst

---

[10] A complete description is given in Chapter VII.

[11] The meaning of these sentences appeared in Section III.4. Fillmore's base appeared in Section IV. 2. For symbols, refer to Appendix II.

[12] VI does not correspond to the verb as defined by traditional Arabic grammar.

[13] Ag$_1$ and Ag$_1$ refer to the same agent.

15. bi ?al qalami + katab   + ?al waladu
         Inst   + Aux Vl +   Ag

16. 9ala ?al Ta:wilati + kita:bun
          Loc   +   Erg

17. busta:nu ?al bayti + kabi:run
           Erg   + Aux Vl

18. ?al baytu busta:nuhu + kabi:run
           Erg   + Aux Vl

19. maša
     Aux Vl

20. ma + maša + sami:run
     Neg + Aux Vl + Ag

21. ka:na + ?al baytu + jami:lan
      Aux +   Erg   + Vl

22. sa:ra   + sami:run + wa ?al nahra
     Aux Vl +   Ag   +   S

23. waqafa + sami:run   + ?ihtra:man li ?al mu9allimi
     Aux Vl +   Ag   +   S

24. waqafa   + sami:run   + Da:hikan
     Aux Vl +   Ag   +   S

25. 9umaru + huwa + ?al 9a:dilu
      Ag   +   +   Vl[14]

26. la: + ?ahada + fi: ?al dari
     Neg + Erg   +   Loc

27. ?rui:du + ?an ?aktuba
     Aux Vl +   S

28. lam + yatub   + ?al waladu
     Neg + Aux Vl +   Ag

29. kutibat + ?al risa:latu
     Aux Vl +   Erg

30. ?inna + ?al waladayni + wasi:ma:ni
     Mod +   Erg   +   Vl

31. la: + Walada + fi: ?al bayti
     Neg+ Erg   + Loc

32. ka:da + ?al waladu + yamši:
     Aux +   Ag   + Vl

----

[14] Slots that are kept empty indicate that the word cannot be accounted for by PS-rules. It is the function of the coming T-rules in Chapter VI to account for them.

33. maša   + mašyan
     Aux Vl + Emph
34. ?inna + sami:ran + ka:tibun + darsahu
     Mod   +   Ag   +   Vl   +   Erg
35. ?al risa:latu + maktu:batun
            Erg   +   Vl
36. ma: + ?aǰmala + ?al bayta
     Ag + Aux Vl +   Erg
37. ?al bayta + ya: sami:ru
         Erg   +   S
38. ?iyya:ka + wa ?al na:ra
         Erg   +   S
39. sami:run + ?aTwalu + min layala:
          Ag   +   Vl   +   Erg
40. kataba + ?al ?wla:du + ?illa: sami:ran
     Aux Vl +   Ag   +   S
41. kita:batu ?al waladi + ǰami:latun
            Erg   +   Vl
42. fataḥa + ?al mifta:ḥu + ?al ba:ba ?al ?aḥmara
     Aux Vl +   Inst   +   Erg
43. maša: + ?al waladu + nafsuhu
     Aux Vl +   Ag   +
44. maša: + ?al waladu sami:run + ?amsi
     Aux Vl +   Ag   + Tadv
45. ma: + ?ismuka
     Q   +   Erg
46. ?inqaTa9a + ?al ḥablu ?alaði: ?štaray ta ḥu
         Aux Vl   +   Erg
47. maša   + sami:run wa 9aliyyun + huna
     Aux Vl +   Ag   + Loc
48. ?ala + tusa:9idun + i:
     Q   + Aux Vl   + Erg
49. ?a + maša: + ?al waladu[15]
     Q   + Aux Vl +   Ag
50. ha:ða waladun + sa:fara + ?abu:hu
         Erg   + Aux Vl +   Ag

---

[15] *?a* is chosen instead of *hal* because *?a* can question verbal, nominal, negative, or affirmative sentences whereas *hal* cannot be used except with affirmative ones.

51.   ?uktub + ?al darsa
      Aux Vl +   Erg
52.   ?in + tadrus + tanjah
      Mod + S_1 + S_2

These descriptions of the previous sentences are not meant to be detailed or complete. The purpose has been merely to get a further quick clue of the suitability of Fillmore's model to Arabic. However, as far as these tentative descriptions tell and with the assumption that the corpus is highly representative, one may conclude that Fillmore's base can fairly satisfactorily account for the deep structure of Arabic.

CHAPTER FIVE

LEXICAL RULES

V.1. *Introduction*

After applying the PS-rules, one has to apply the lexical (L) rules to complete the determination of meaning that was started in the PS-rules: the PS-rules supply the underlying functions but the L-rules supply the lexical entities that perform those functions. Further, these L-rules contain a variety of features that are needed in the syntactic, semantic, and phonological components of a language. They may even contain information usable in the area of graphics.

In addition, the L-rules solve the problem of selectional restrictions which is not solved by the PS-rules in Section IV. 2. The L-rules specify for every noun, verbal, and other constituents of the base the necessary features that solve the problem of which noun goes with which verbal. Of course, such features cannot go in the PS-rules, which have to be broad and general, nor can they go in the T-rules, which process the input into an output. The only place where these features can be put is the L-rules.

This explains why the grammar does not allow *?al baytu kataba ?al darsa* because *kataba* has a human-agent feature and *?al bayt* does not meet this requirement.

The features in the lexicon are marked with + to mean a positive feature, with − to mean a negative one, i.e., the absence of that feature, or with to ∓ mean either positive or negative. However, the absence of a feature usually implies the presence of another one: e.g., - masculine means + feminine.

Further, features in general may imply other features, which is responsible for introducing the concept of "redundancy".[1] The feature + pronoun implies + noun; the feature + human implies + animate. These are examples; a detailed discussion of redundancy will come in the following sections of this chapter.

---
[1] Noam Chomsky, *Aspects of the Theory of Syntax*, p. 164.

The L-rules of this chapter describe only the lexical items that appear in the corpus, to which all the thesis is limited. Every category of words appear in a separate section: + nouns, + verbals, + determiners, + prepositions, + interrogatives, + negatives, + auxiliaries, and + time adverbials. The symbol for each category is written as a capital letter whereas the symbols for other features are written in small letters.

V.2.   *Plus Noun (+N) Words*

In describing these words, many symbols are used to stand for significant features.

1.   N: All words in this section are nouns; this N comes from the PS-rules. All words here are + N.

2.   pro = pronoun. *kita:b* is − pro, but *huwa* is + pro though both are + N. This pro feature is needed in T-rules which deal with copying and pronominalization, e.g., T29 and T14.

3.   anim = animate. *kita:b* is − anim, but *walad* is + anim. This feature is necessary for selectional restrictions: some verbs have to take + anim agents such as *šariba* or *maša: ?al kita:b* is not allowed.

4.   hum = human. *ba:b* is − hum, but walad is + hum. This feature is necessary for selectional restrictions as well. Some verbs must go with + hum or − hum agents; that is why *kataba ?al ba:bu* is not allowed, whereas *kataba ?alwaladu* is.

5.   con = concrete. This feature means "touchable" or "substantial" versus abstract. *ba:b* is con but *huwa* which stands for an abstract such as *suru:r* "pleasure" is − con. This feature is necessary for selection: *šariba* "drank" must have a concrete object; *šariba ?al suru:ra* is not allowed.

6.   com = common. mifta: ħ "key" is + com, but *sami:r* is − com, i.e., proper. This distinction is necessary because + com takes *?al* but − com does not. In fact, *?al* is the test of ∓ com: if a noun need *?al* to be definite, it is + com; if it does not, it is − com.

7.   count = countable. *walad* is + count, but *ma:?* "water" is − count. The test for this is taking numbers, i.e., countability. This distinction is necessary for selection restrictions: − count cannot take numbers with it nor can it be dualized or pluralized.

8.   sing = singular, e.g., *walad*

9.   d = dual, *e.g., walada:n*

10. pl = plural e.g., *?awla:d*. The last three features are necessary for verbal agreement and pronominalization.

11. def = definite. *kita:b* is – def, but *sami:r* is + def. This is tested by adding an adjective: if the adjective has *?al*, the noun is + def; if the adjective takes no *?al*, the noun is – def. This distinction is essential for determining adjectives and the *mubtada?*-slot noun, because – def cannot occupy such a slot.

12. masc = masculine, not feminine. *kita:b* is + masc but *Ta:wilat* is – masc. The test for this is *huwa* for + masc and *hiya* for – masc. The distinction is certainly important for verbal agreement and pronominalization.

13. I = first person, e.g., *?ana* "I"

14. II = second person, e.g., *?anta* "you"

15. III = third person, e.g., *huwa* "he". The last three features are determined for pronouns easily, but for nouns that are – pro the feature depends on the situation. However, if the noun is – hum, the feature cannot be except + III. These person features are necessary for verbal agreement transformation.

16. infl = inflected. If the noun accepts several case ending as its position requires, it is + infl, e.g., *kita:b*, which may be *kita:bun*, *kita:ban*, or *kita:bin*. However, if the noun does not show except the form it has in the lexicon regardless of its position in the sentence, it is – infl. e.g., *layla, huwa,* and *ha:ða*. This distinction is necessary in the case introduction transformation (T 16).

17. sep = separable. If the noun is free, it is + sep e.g., *walad*. If the noun is bound to another word both graphically and syntactically, it is – sep, e.g., *ta* in *katabta* "you wrote" versus *kataba ?al waladu*. When *?al waladu kataba* is allowed, *ta kataba* is not allowed.

18. nom = nominative. + nom indicates that the noun occupies a *mubtada?* slot or a *fa:9il* slot, e.g., *huwa*.

19. acc = accusative. +acc indicates that the noun occupies an object slot or modifies an object, e.g., *?iyya:ka*.

20. gen = genitive. +gen indicates that the noun occupies a slot preceded by a preposition or occupies the second slot of a possessive construct, e.g., *fi: baytin*.

21. – nom = accusative or genitive, e.g., *i:* "me".

22. ∓ nom = accusative, nominative, or genitive. This indicates that this lexical unit can be in any case slot and take any case ending, e.g., *kita:b*.

In the above-mentioned features, one sees the following redundancy rules:[2]

+	human	⊃ +	animate	
−	animate	⊃ −	human	
−	concrete	⊃ −	countable	
+	common	⊃ −	definite	
−	common	⊃ +	definite	
+	countable	⊃ +	common	
+	countable	⊃ +	concrete	
+	plural	⊃ +	countable	
+	dual	⊃ +	countable	
−	definite	⊃ +	common	
−	human	⊃ +	third person	
∓	nominative	⊃ +	inflected	

In spite of these redundancy rules, each word is made to have most of those features for the sake of consistency. Here is a table of + N words and their features:

(1)	kita:b	(2)	Ta:wilat	(3)	mifta:ḥ	(4)	ba:b
	kita:b		Ta:wilat		mifta:ḥ		ba:b
	"book"		"table"		"key"		"door"
+	N	+	N	+	N	+	N
−	pro	−	pro	−	pro	−	pro
−	anim	−	anim	−	anim	−	anim
−	hum	−	hum	−	hum	−	hum
+	con	+	con	+	con	+	con
+	com	+	com	+	com	+	com
+	count	+	count	+	count	+	count
+	sing	+	sing	+	sing	+	sing
−	def	−	def	−	def	−	def
+	masc	−	masc	+	masc	+	masc
+	III	+	III	+	III	+	III
+	infl	+	infl	+	infl	+	infl
+	sep[3]	+	sep	+	sep	+	sep
∓	nom	∓	nom	∓	nom	∓	nom

---

[2] The symbol ⊃ = implies

[3] The term "separable" is preferred to "affix" because an affix becomes very closely related to the stem and shows almost no relation to what is outside the stem, e.g., *?istaq*dama and kata*btu: ?st* is an affix because it has become a part of the word but *tu* "I" is not an affix because it is still external to the word. In fact, *?istaqdama* is a word but *katabtu* is a sentence with *tu* as agentive.

(5)	walad	(6)	sami:r	(7)	ħabl	(8)	qalam

walad	sami:r	ħabl	qalam
"boy"	"Sameer"	"rope"	"pen"
+ N	+ N	+ N	+ N
− pro	− pro	− pro	− pro
+ anim	+ anim	− anim	− anim
+ hum	+ hum	− hum	− hum
+ con	+ con	+ con	+ con
+ com	− com	+ com	+ com
+ count	+ count	+ count	+ count
+ sing	+ sing	+ sing	+ sing
− def	+ def	− def	− def
+ masc	+ masc	+ masc	+ masc
+ III	+ III	+ III	+ III
+ infl	+ infl	+ infl	+ infl
+ sep	+ sep	+ sep	+ sep
∓ nom	∓ nom	∓ nom	∓ nom

(9)	huna	(10)	ha:ða	(11)	huwa	(12)	busta:n

huna:	ha:ða	huwa	busta:n
"here"	"this"	"huwa"	"garden"
+ N	+ N	+ N	+ N
− pro	− pro	+ pro	− pro
− anim	∓ anim[5]	∓ anim	− anim
− hum	∓ hum	∓ hum	− hum
+ con	∓ con	∓ con	+ con
− com	+ com	∓ com	+ com
− count	∓ count	∓ count	+ count
+ def	+ sing	+ sing	+ sing
− number[4]	+ def	+ def	− def
− gender	+ masc	+ masc	+ masc
− infl	+ III	+ III	+ III
+ sep	− infl	− infl	+ infl
− nom	+ demonstrative	+ sep	+ sep
+ locative	+ sep	+ noun	+ nom
	∓ nom		∓ nom

---

[4] This word has no number, person, or gender.

[5] The feature of anim, hum, con, and count for *ha:ða* depend on what the word stands for. If it stands for +anim, it is +anim etc. So is the case with all pronouns: such features are determined by the noun they refer to.

(13) bayt   (14) layla: (15) nahr   (16) 9umar

bayt   layla: nahr   9umar

"house"   "Laila"   "river"   "Omar"
+ N   + N   + N   + N
− pro   − pro   − pro   − pro
− anim   + anim   − anim   + anim
− hum   + hum   − hum   + hum
+ con   + con   + con   + con
+ com   − com   + com   − com
+ count   + count   + count   + count
+ sing   + sing   + sing   + sing
− def   + def   − def   + def
+ masc   − masc   + masc   + masc
+ III   + III   + III   + III
+ infl   − infl   + infl   + infl
+ sep   + sep   + +   + +
∓ nom   ∓ nom   ∓ nom   ∓ nom

(17) ?aħad   (18) risa:lat   (19) dars   (20) ma:

?aħad   risa:lat   dars   ma:

"person"   "letter"   "lesson"   "something"
+ N   + N   + N   + N
− pro   − pro   − pro   + pro
+ anim   − anim   − anim   − anim
+ hum   − hum   − hum   − hum
+ con   + con   + con   + con
+ com   + com   + com   + com
+ count   + count   + count   − count
+ sing   + sing   + sing   + sing
− def   − def   − def   − def
+ masc   − masc   + masc   + masc
+ III   + III   + III   + III
+ infl   + infl   + infl   − infl
+ sep   + sep   + sep   + sep
∓ nom   ∓ nom   ∓ nom   ∓ nom

(21) ?iyya:ka   (22) na:r   (23) waladayni   (24) ?awla:d

?iyya:ka   na:r   waladayni   ?awla:d

"you"   "fire"   "two boys"   "boys"
+ N   + N   + N   + N
+ pro   − pro   − pro   − pro

+ anim	− anim	+ anim	− anim
+ hum	− hum	+ hum	− hum
+ con	+ con	+ con	+ con
− com	+ com	+ com	+ com
+ count	− count	+ count	− count
+ sing	+ sing	+ d	+ sing
+ def	− def	− def	− def
+ masc	− masc	+ masc	+ masc
+ II	+ III	+ III	+ III
− infl	+ infl	+ infl	− infl
+ sep	+ sep	+ sep	+ sep
+ acc	∓ nom	− nom	∓ nom

(25) kita:bat   (26) nafsuhu   (27) ma: (28) ?ism

kita:bat	nafsuhu	ma:	?ism
"writing"	"himself or itself"	"what"	"name"
+ N	+ N	+ N	+ N
− pro	+ pro	+ pro	+ pro
− anim	∓ anim	∓ anim	− anim
− hum	∓ hum	− hum	− hum
+ con	∓ con	∓ con	+ con
+ com	∓ com	∓ com	+ com
− count	+ count	− count	− count
+ sing	+ sing	+ sing	+ sing
− def	+ def	+ def	− def
+ masc	+ masc	+ masc	+ masc
+ III	+ III	+ III	+ III
+ infl	+ infl	− infl	− infl
+ sep	+ sep	+ sep	+ sep
∓ nom	+ nom	∓ nom	∓ nom
		+ interrogative	

(29) ?allaði: (30) ta   (23) hu   (24) 9aliyy

?allaði:	ta	hu	9aliyy
"who, which"	"you"	"it, him"	"Ali"
+ N	+ N	+ N	+ N
+ pro	+ pro	+ pro	− pro
∓ anim	+ anim	∓ anim	+ anim
∓ hum	+ hum	∓ hum	+ hum
∓ con	+ con	+ con	+ con
∓ com	− com	∓ com	− com
∓ count	+ count	∓ count	+ count

+ sing	+ sing	+ sing	+ sing
+ def	+ def	+ def	+ def
+ masc	+ masc	+ masc	+ masc
∓ II	+ II	+ III	+ III
− infl	− infl	− infl	+ infl
+ sep	− sep	− sep	+ sep
∓ nom	+ nom	− nom	∓ nom
+ relative			

(33) i: (34) ?ab

i: ?ab

"me"   "father"
+ N   + N
+ pro   − pro
+ anim   + anim
+ hum   + hum
+ con   + con
− com   + com
+ count   + count
+ sing   + sing
+ def   − def
∓ masc   + masc
+ I   + III
− infl   + infl
− sep   + sep
− nom   ∓ nom

V.3.   *Plus Verbal* (+Vl) *Words*

In this section, the following features will be used:

1.   Vl = verbal. Verbals are supplied as a category by PS-rules.

2.   V = verb. *kataba* is + V, but *ka:tib* is − V though both are +Vl. The test for the + V or − V is that − V behaves partly like + N words but + V does not: *katib* takes case endings as a noun does, e.g., *ka:tibun, ka:tiban,* and *ka:tibin*. In fact, these − V verbals are very difficult to deal with because of their behaviour; they may take objects like verbs and do take case endings like nouns, e.g., *huwa ka:tibun darsan*. However, it has been decided to regard such words as verbals rather than nouns to the advantage of the grammar simplicity and adequacy. Further, *ka:tibun* can be easily changed into *kataba* or

yaktubu without affecting meaning or syntax. This proves that the underlying function of *ka:tibun* is verbal and not nominal.

3. act = action. A verbal is + act if it can be made imperative and still remain acceptable, e.g., *kataba* is + act because *?uktub* is acceptable. On the other hand, *Tawi:l* "tall" is – act, because the imperative *Tul* is unacceptable.

4. tr = transitive. A verbal is +tr if it takes an object, e.g., *?a9Ta:*"gave". A verbal is –tr if it does not take an object, e.g., *maša:*.

5. inst = instrument. A verbal is ∓ inst if it may need an instrument, e.g., *aqTa9a* "cut". In fact, no verbal in this section is +inst in the sense that it must have an instrument because the instrument noun phrase is mainly optional. However, there are verbals that are – inst, which means that they cannot have an instrument noun phrase, e.g., *kabura* "grew".

6. hum Ag = human agent. A verbal is +hum Ag if it takes a human agent, e.g., *kataba*.

7. anim Ag = animate agent. A verbal is +anim Ag if it takes an animate agent, e.g., *qata9a*, the agent of which may be a dog or a boy.

8. anim Erg = animate ergative. A verbal is ∓ anim Erg if it may take an ergative that is +anim or –anim, e.g.,*?uri:du kita:ban* "I want a book" or *?uri:du kalban* "I want a dog". A verbal is ∓hum Erg if it may take an ergative that is +hum or –hum, e.g., *?iħtarama ?al 9alama* "he respected the flag" and *?iħtaram ?aba:hu* "he respected his father". A verbal is –anim Erg if it takes an inanimate ergative, e.g.,*fataħa ?al ba:ba* "he opened the door".

9. masc = masculine. All verbals that are +V are +masc in the form they have in the lexicon in the sense that they match with masculine agents or ergatives, e.g., *maša:*. However, –V verbals may be +masc such as kabi:r "large", -masc such as *ǰami:lat* "beautiful", or ∓ masc such as *?aTwal* "taller".

10. Dat = dative. A verbal is +Dat if it takes a dative noun phrase, e.g., *?a9Ta:* "gave"

Using these features, here is a description of the verbals of the corpus:

(1) qaTa9a   (2)   kabura   (3)   Daħu:k   (4)   kataba

qaTa9a	kabura	Daħu:k	kataba
"cut"	"grew"	"cheerful"	"wrote"
+ Vl	+ Vl	+ Vl	+ Vl

+ V	+ V	– V	+ v
+ act	– act	+ act	+ act
+ tr	– tr	– tr	+ tr
∓ inst	– inst	– inst	∓ inst
+ anim Ag	∓ anim Erg	+ hum Ag	+ hum Ag
– anim Erg	+ masc	∓ masc[7]	– anim Erg
+ masc[6]			+ masc

(5) ?a9Ta: (6) ?inqaTa9a   (7) fataħa   (8) maša:

?a9Ta	?inqaTa9a	fataħa	maša:
"gave"	"separated"	"opened"	"walked"
+ Vl	+ Vl	+ Vl	+ Vl
+ V	+ V	– V	+ V
+ act	– act	+ act	+ act
+ tr	– tr	– tr	– tr
∓ inst	∓ inst	– inst	– inst
+ anim Ag	– anim Erg	+ hum Ag	+ anim Ag
– anim Erg	+ masc	∓ masc	+ masc
+ Dat			
+ masc			

(9) kabi:r   (10) ǰami:l   (11) sa:ra   (12) waqafa

kabir	ǰami:l	sa:ra	waqafa
"large"	"pretty"	"walked"	"stood up"
+ Vl	+ Vl	+ Vl	+ Vl
– V	– V	+ V	+ V
– act	– act	+ act	+ act
– tr	– tr	– tr	– tr
– inst	– inst	– inst	– inst
∓ anim Erg	∓ anim Erg	+ anim Ag	+ anim Ag
+ masc	+ masc	+ masc	+ masc

(13) ?iħtira:m   (14) Da:ħik   (15) 9a:dil   (16) ?ara:da

?iħtira:m	Da:ħik	9a:dil	?ara:da
"respect"	"laughing"	"just"	"wanted"

---

[6] All +V verbals are in the past form. Other forms are to be supplied by M-rules, e.g.,

    Press + qaTa9a → yaqTa9u

[7] Case endings of –V verbals do not appear here because they depend on position and environment.

+ Vl	+ Vl	+ Vl	+ Vl
− V	− V	− V	+ V
+ act	+ act	+ act	+ act
+ tr	− tr	− tr	+ tr
− inst	− inst	− inst	− inst
+ hum Ag	+ hum Ag	+ hum Ag	+ anim Ag
∓ hum Erg	+ masc	+ masc	∓ anim Erg
+ masc			+ masc

(17) ka:tib (18) maktu:bat (19) ?ajmala (20) ?aTwal

ka:tib	maktu:bat	?ajmala	?aTwal
"writing"	"written"	"beautify"	"taller"
+ Vl	+ Vl	+ Vl	+ Vl
− V	− V	+ V	+ V
+ act	+ act	+ act	+ act
+ tr	− tr	+ tr	− tr
∓ inst	∓ inst	− inst	− inst
+ anim Erg	+ hum Ag	− anim Ag	+ anim Ag
− anim Erg	− anim Erg	∓ anim Erg	+ masc
+ masc	− masc	+ masc	+ comparative

(21) jami:lat (22) ?ahmar (23) ištara: (24) sa:9ada

jami:lat	?ahmar	ištara:	sa9ada
"beautiful"	"red"	"bought"	"helped"
+ Vl	+ Vl	+ Vl	+ Vl
− V	− V	+ V	+ V
− act	− act	+ act	+ act
− tr	− tr	+ tr	+ tr
− inst	− inst	∓ inst	∓ inst
∓ anim Erg	∓ anim Erg	+ hum Ag	∓ anim Ag
− masc	+ masc	− anim Erg	∓ anim Erg
		+ masc	+ masc

(25) sa:fara (26) darasa (27) najaha (28) ra?a:

sa:fara	darasa	najaha	ra?a:
"travelled"	"studied"	"succeeded"	"saw"
+ Vl	+ Vl	+ Vl	+ Vl
+ V	+ V	+ V	+ V
+ act	+ act	+ act	+ act
− tr	+ tr	− tr	+ tr
− inst	− inst	− inst	∓ inst

+ hum Ag	+ hum Ag	+ hum Ag	+ anim Ag
+ masc	∓ hum Erg	+ masc	∓ anim Erg
	+ masc		+ masc

V.4. *Plus Determiners* (+ Det)

In describing determiners, the following features will be used:

1.   def = definite. *?al* in *?al kita:b* is +def, but *waladin* in *kita:bu waladin* is –def. Although *walad* is +N, it may have a determiner function. These are two arguments for considering *waladin* here as +Det, and not +N. Firstly, *waladin* resembles *?al* in making *kita:b* definite. Secondly, *waladin* and *?al* are in complementary distribution; they cannot occur together in *?al kita:bu waladin*. The alternative solution is to derive *kita:bu waladin* from *waladun yamliku kita:ban* "a boy has a book". But this solution complicates the grammar rather than simplifies it or, to put it differently, it is less simple than the first solution.

2.   poss = possessive. *?al* is –poss, but *waladin* in *kita:bu waladin* is +poss. However, the term "possessive" does not always literally mean possession; the relation may be temporal, e.g., *dursu ?al Saba:ħi* "a morning lesson", object, e.g., *ka:tib darsihi* "writing his lesson", or material, e.g., *baytu zuǰaǰin* "a house of glass". The term "possessive" is made here a blanket term to cover all other relations.

3.   sep = separable. *waladin* is +sep, but *?al* is –sep, which means that *waladin* is a free form but *?al* is a bound form. This distinction is necessary for the determiner transformation that will be dealt with in the coming chapter.

4.   suff = suffix. *?al* is –suff, but *hu* in *kita:buhu* "his book" is +suff. The term "suffix" here merely means "put after". This information is certainly useful for both T-rules and M-rules.

5.   gen = genitive. *waladin* in *kita:bu waladin* is +gen, but *?al* in *?al kita:bu* is –gen. The feature +gen means the genitive case ending *in* or *i*. However, –gen does not mean nominative or accusative; it only means that it is not genitive and, in fact, not any other case ending. In addition, there are here two redundancy rules: –gen implies –poss and +gen implies +poss.

(1)	?al	(2)	hu	(3)	ka
	?al		hu		ka
	"the"		"his"		"your"

+	Det	+	Det	+	Det
+	def	+	def	+	def
−	poss	+	poss	+	poss
−	sep	−	sep	−	sep
−	suff	+	suff	+	suff
−	gen	+	gen	+	gen

V.5.   *Plus Prepositions* (+P)

In describing prepositions, the following features are used:

1.   sep = separable. *9ala* "on" is +sep, but *bi* is −sep. A separable preposition is separately in the graphic representation of the language, but an inseparable preposition is attached to the noun after it. A feature that show prefixation is not necessary because the fact that a preposition precedes its noun is supplied by the PS-rules of Fillmore's model.

2.   loc = location. *9ala* as used in the corpus in *?al kita:bu 9ala ?al Ta:wilati* is +loc, but *bi* in *kataba bi ?al qalami* is −loc.

3.   inst   = instrument. *bi* in *kataba bi ?al qalmi* is +inst but *9ala* is −inst.

It is necessary, however, to say that these prepositions described in this section are described as they appear in the corpus and not in absolute manner, e.g., *min* is described as +loc and *bi* as +inst. It is known that they can mean a variety of things in different contexts, but in this context each means one thing.

Further it may be thought that some prepositions can be regarded as parts of two-words forms. But the argument for such a preposition is weak. If *bi* is taken as part of *kataba* in *kataba bi ?al qalami*, two deletions are needed to account for *kataba:* one to delete the noun and one to delete the preposition. Without such a proposition, one deletion of the whole nominal phrase *bi ?al qalmi* is needed, which is simpler than needing two deletions.

The prepositions that appear in the corpus are:

(1) 9ala	(2) fi:	(3) bi	(4) min
9ala	fi:	bi	min
"on"	"in"	"with"	"from"
+ P	+ P	+ P	+ P
+ sep	+ sep	− sep	+ sep
+ loc	+ loc	+ inst	+ loc

V.6. *Plus Interrogative* (+Inter)

This section presents the feature of the interrogatives that appear in the corpus. The features that will be used are;

1. sep = separable. *?a* is –sep but *?ala:* s +sep graphically speaking.

2. req = request. *?a* is –req but *?ala* is +req.

The symbol = / indicates "provided that it is followed by".

(1) ?ala:	(2) ?a
?ala:	?a
"will...please"	"do, did, are?"
+ Inter	Inter
+ sep	– sep
+ req	– req
= /+ v^8	

V.7. *Plus Negatives* (+ Neg)

(1) ma:	(2) la:	(3) lam
ma	la:	"not"
+ Neg	+ Neg	+ Neg
	$=/\begin{cases} -\text{def acc N} \\ +v \end{cases}$	=/ + v jussive past Aux

?ma: can be followed by a verb or a noun, but *la:* must be followed by a nondefinite accusative noun or a verb. As for *lam*, it must be followed by a verb in the jussive present form when the auxiliary is past.

V.8. *Plus Auxiliaries* (+ Aux)

In describing auxiliaries, the following features are used:

1. past: *k:na* is +past, but *yaku:nu* is –past. The main distinction is made between past and nonpast because the nonpast can be used to express the present and the future.

2. modal: *ka:na* is –modal, but *ka:da* is +modal because it carries meaning in addition to tense whereas *ka:na* does not carry except tense. However, "modal" must not be confused with "modality", which

---

[8] *?ala:* must be followed by a verb, but *?a* need not.

dominates sentence adverbials, time adverbials, interrogatives, and negatives as shown by PS in Fillmore's base in Section IV.2.

3. nom N: the noun that follows *ka:na* or *yaku:nu* must be made to have a nominative case ending, e.g., *ka:na ?al waladu mawʄu:dan huna.*

4. acc predicate: the word that informs about the first noun is to be put in the accusative as in the previous examples.

(1) ka:na	(2) yaku:nu	(3) kada
ka:na	yaku:nu	ka:da
"was"	"is"	+ Aux
+ Aux	+ Aux	+ past
+ past	– past	+ modal
–modal	– modal	+ nom N
+ nom N	+ nom N	+ present verb
+ acc Predicate	+ acc Predicate	predicate

The reasons why *ka:na* is taken as an auxiliary and not as Vl are multiple. Firstly, it is mainly a tense-carrier, which should be a function of the auxiliary. Secondly, the deletability of *yaku:n* shows that it cannot be a verbal, which is an essential element in the sentence that should not be deleted. Thirdly, some verbals are optionally deleted but *yaku:n* is deleted obligatorily as shown in T-rules next chapter. Fourthly, it often appears with other verbals, e.g., *?al waldu ka:na yamši:* All these prove that there are strong arguments for considering *ka:na* and *yaku:nu* as auxiliaries and not as verbals.

V.9. *Plus Time Adverbials* (+Tadv)

There is only one time adverbial in the corpus:

?amsi

?amsi

"yesterday"
+ Tadv
+ past

CHAPTER SIX

TRANSFORMATIONAL RULES
(T-RULES)

To recapitulate briefly what was covered in Section II.7, a transformation is a process that converts a deep structure, where meaning is determined through PS-rules, into an intermediate or surface structure, where form is determined. For details about transformation rules (T-rules), one may refer to section I.7, where there is a long discussion on the nature, function, condition, order, and types of T-rules.

In this chapter, there will be an attempt to design the T-rules that are needed to convert the deep structures into surface one. Every T-rule will be given a number and described as obligatory (OBL) or optional (OPT). Further, it will be given a name and explained in ordinary language. Then there will be a structural description (SD) of the input of the T-rule. This SD will be followed by a structural change (SC) expressed in both symbols and figures. The structural change is followed by the conditions for applying the T-rule, if there are such conditions; this mean talking about the ordering of T-rules. Afterwards, there will be one or more examples of that rule. Then there will be a record of some sentences in the corpus that need such a T-rule. This will be followed by a general discussion. Finally, there will be a brief comparison between Arabic and English concerning that T-rule.

In brief, every T-rule in this chapter will have a number, OBL or OPT, name, explanation, SD, SC, condition, example, application, discussion, and a comparison.

The PS-rules that will supply the deep structure are those of Fillmore's modified model as presented in Sections IV.2. and IV.3:

PS1: S → (Mod) Aux Prop

PS2: Mod → $\begin{Bmatrix} \text{SentenceAdverbial} \\ \text{Time Adverbials} \\ \text{Interrogatives} \\ \text{NegativeElements} \end{Bmatrix}$

PS3: Prop → Vl (Erg) (Dat) (Loc) (Inst) (Ag)

$$PS4: \quad \begin{bmatrix} Erg \\ Dat \\ Loc \\ Inst \\ Ag \end{bmatrix} \rightarrow NP$$

PS5: NP → P (Det) N (S)

Tl (OBL):   *Subject Preposition Deletion*

This obligatory transformation deletes the preposition of NP when the noun functions as a surface subject, which corresponds to *mubtada?* or *fa:9il* in traditional Arabic grammar, e.g., *?al waladu maša:* and *maša: ?al waladu.*

Structural Description (SD): Aux⌢V + P + X⌢N

where X is a cover symbol that stands for anything allowed by the grammar to occupy that slot, and the sing ⌢ makes the two symbol on both sides a unit in this instance.

This SD is essential as a condition for applying the T-rule: it proves the analysability of the structure in line with the PS-rules.

Structural Change (SC): Aux⌢V + Ø + X⌢N
$$1 + 2 + 3 \Rightarrow 1 + Ø + 3$$
where double arrow ⇒ means "is transformed into" and Ø means zero after deletion.

Condition: N is surface subject.

Example: maša: + min + ?al walad[1]
⇒ maša: + Ø + ?al walad

Application: This rule has to be applied to most sentences in the corpus, e.g., 51, 52, S33 and S4.

Discussion: One may ask why the preposition is there if it is to be deleted later. If the base does not include P, it would complicate the rules to introduce it when it is needed with a nominalized verb, e.g.,

---

[1] Case endings are supplied by another T-rule.

All sentences hereafter will appear without a preposition (P) before the surface subject except when P is needed.

The sequence of T-rules in this chapter does not necessarily correspond to their sequence in application. However, their order in application will be shown in Chapter VI, where the grammar efficiency is tested.

?al mašy *min*?al walad, ?al ?i9Ta:? *li* ?al walad, ?al kita:bat *bi* ?al qalam, and ?al qat9 *li* ?al ḥabl to exemplify NP's that are an agent, dative, instrument, and ergative respectively.

This rule involves the selection of the subject, which in turn puts restrictions on what constituents of Prop can go together: *fataḥa ?al mifta:ḥu ?al ba:ba min ?al waladi* is not allowed. Here is a list of these restrictions; the subject is placed after Vl:

(1) Vl Erg (Loc), e.g., *kutibat ?al risa:latu (huna:)*
(2) Vl Erg Dat (Loc), e.g., *?u9Tiya Kita:bun la hu (huna:)*
(3) Vl Dat Erg (Ag) (Loc), e.g., *?u9Tiya sami:run kita:ban (min ?al waldi) (huna:)*
(4) Vl Inst Erg, e.g., *fataḥa ?al mifta:ḥu ?al ba:ba*
(5) Vl Ag (Loc), e.g., *maša: ?al waladu (huna:)*
(6) Vl Ag Erg (Loc), e.g., *fataḥa ?al waladu ?al ba:ba (huna:)*
(7) Vl Ag Inst (Loc), e.g., *kataba ?al waladu bi ?al qalami (huna:)*
(8) Vl Ag Erg Dat (Loc), e.g., *?a9Ta: ?al waladu kita:ban li sami:rin (huna:)*
(9) Vl Ag Erg (Inst) (Loc), e.g., *fataḥa ?al waladu ?al ba:ba (bi ?al mifta:hi) (huna:)*

Comparison: There is a similar T-rule in English which obligatorily deletes P of NP where N is a surface subject:[2]
by + the boy + walked $\Rightarrow$ Ø + the boy + walked[3]

The argument for assuming "by" assumed instead as coming from the boy". However, "of" can be assumed instead as coming from "the walking of the boy".

T2 (OBL):   *Object Preposition Deletion*

This rule deletes the preposition of the nominal phrase (NP) when the noun functions as an object. In this case, N is dominated by Erg or fronted Dat and not by Ag, Inst, or Loc.[4] In other words, this rule will apply to the direct object and the fronted indirect object, i.e., the dative, e.g., *?a9Ta: ?al walad sami:r kita:b.*

---

[2] Charles Fillmore, "A Proposal Concerning English Prepositions", *Monograph Series on Language and Linguistics,* No. 19, p. 31.

[3] The English example in discussions and comparisons need not begin with capital letters because they may be ungrammatical fragments of sentences.

[4] For abbreviations, see Appendix III.

SD: Aux⌢V⌢X + P + Y⌢N
        where X and Y are cover symbols.
SC: Aux⌢V⌢X + Ø + Y⌢N
        1 + 2 + 3 ⇒ 1 + Ø + 3

Condition: N is the object of V

Example: fataħa ?al mifta:ħ + li + ?al ba:b
        ⇒   fataħa ?al mifta:ħ + Ø + ?al ba:b[5]

Application: This rule has to be applied in S2, S4, S5 and several
        others.[6]

Discussion: Without assuming the existence of *li* before the noun
        when NP is ergative or dative, it would be difficult to explain
        fatħu ?a mifta:ħi li ?al ba:bi, where *li* appears before the ergative,
        or *?i9Ta:a:? ?al kita:b li sami:r*, where *li* appears before the dative.
        Further, one may suggest to condense T1 and T2 into one rule.
        But because each has a different SD and a different condition, it
        is better to keep them as two separate rules.

Comparison: In English there is a similar T-rule:
        the key opened + of + the door.
        ⇒ the key opened + Ø + the door.

T3 (OBL):   *yaku:n Deletion*

This rule obligatorily deletes *yaku:n*. However the rule does not apply
to *ka:na* "was". This rule will help to account for nominal sentences
such as *?al kita:b 9ala ?al Ta:wilat*.

SD: yaku:n + V1⌢$_{-v}$Erg⌢X[7]
SC: Ø   + V1⌢$_{-v}$Erg⌢X
           1 + 2 ⇒ Ø + 2

Condition: There is no external condition; it is what SD says, V1$_{-v}$
        is a verbal that is not a verb, i.e., jamĭ:l or mawǰu:d.

---

[5] All sentences hereafter will appear without a preposition before the object, which
covers the ergative and the dative, except when necessary.

[6] These numbers appearing in front of each application all through the T-rules refer
to the numbers of the sentences in the corpus.

[7] There is no need to write Erg as NP$_{Erg}$ implies NP and because Erg
is simpler.

Examples: (1) yaku:n + mawǰu:d ?al kita:b 9ala ?al Ta:wilat
    ⇒ *Ø   + mawǰu:d ?al kita:b 9ala ?al Ta:wilat[8]
    (2) yaku:n + kabi:r   ?al bayt
    ⇒ *Ø   + kabi:r   ?al bayt

Application: S1, S16, S31, and S45.

Discussion: Assuming the existence of *yaku:n* in the base solves many problems:
(1) *yaku:n* is needed after negative particles, e.g., *la: yaku:n mawju:dan.* it would be difficult to introduce it if it is not originally there.
(2) It would be easier to see the symmetry of language. Without *yaku:n*, it would be difficult to assume *ka:na*, e.g., *ka:na ?al walad huna:k.*

Comparison: There is no "b" deletion in English. This explains the negative transfer in the mistake of many Arab students in "the book on the table", where "is" is deleted in wrong analogy of *yaku:n* deletion.[9]

T4 (OPT):   *Ergative-Dative Permutation*

This rule allows Erg and Dat to exchange positions given by PS3: Prop → V1 (Erg) (Dat) (Loc) (Inst) (Ag). It may be called "Indirect Object Inversion". Such a rule is needed to account for such sentences as *?a9Ta: sami:r kita:b* "He have Sameer a book", which is a stylistic variety of *?a9Ta: kita:b ?ila: sami:r* "he gave a book to Sameer".

SD: X͡V + Erg + Dat + Y
SC: X͡V + Erg + Dat + Y
    $1 + 2 + 3 + 4 \Rightarrow 1 + 3 + 2 + 4$

Condition: There is no external condition except the mere existence of Erg and Dat, which implies the existence of a transitive V that takes Dat as well.

Examples: ?a9Ta + kita:b + ?ila   sami:r + Y
    ⇒ *?a9Ta + ?ila: sami:r + kita:b + Y

---

[8] The sign * means that this structure is ungrammatical and needs a further transformation, i.e., it is an intermediate structure.

[9] This deletion exemplifies the phenomenon of the language tendency towards the economy of expression without damaging meaning.

This output is intermediate and T2 has to be applied to produce:

$\Rightarrow$?a9Ta + Ø + sami:r + kita:b + Y

Application: S2.

Discussion: X and Y in the SD stand for any irrelevant strings that may go there. Without them the description would be simpler but less precise.

Comparison: Such a rule is applied optionally also to English sentences:

     he gave + a book + to John
$\Rightarrow$ he gave + to John + a book
$\Rightarrow$ he gave + Ø John + a book

T5 (OBL):   *Ergative or Agent Fronting*

This rule puts Erg or Ag at the beginning of Prop, i.e., before V1, when V1 is $-$v. This rule is needed to produce such sentences as *ka:na 9ummar 9a:dil* "Omar was just". However, if V1 is $+$v, the rule is not needed, e.g., *ka:na yamši: ?al walad*.

SD: Aux + V1$_{-v}$ + $\begin{Bmatrix} \text{Erg} \\ \text{Ag} \end{Bmatrix}$

SC: Aux + $\begin{Bmatrix} \text{Erg} \\ \text{Ag} \end{Bmatrix}$ + V1$_{-v}$

     $1 + 2 + 3 \Rightarrow 1 + 3 + 2$

Condition: V1 is $-$v.

Examples:
    (1)   yaku:n + Daħu:k   + ?al walad
        $\Rightarrow$ *yaku:n + ?al walad + Daħu:k,
    which needs further T-rules such as *yaku:n* Deletion
    (2)   ka:na + 9a:dil + 9umar
        $\Rightarrow$ ka:na + 9umar + 9a:dil

Application: S7, S30, S41.

Discussion: If Erg or Ar is $-$def, T29 (*mubtada?* Copying) must be applied as well:

walad + Daħu:k $\Rightarrow$ huwa + walad + Daħu:k

Comparison: A similar T-rule exists in English:
  is handsome + the boy $\Rightarrow$ the boy + is handsome,
  (1) If N of Erg or Ag is –def, T29 (*mubtada?* Copying) need not
      be applied:
      is useful + a cow $\Rightarrow$ a cow + is useful
  (2) Further, the rule must be applied whether V1 is + v or – v.
      are useful + cows $\Rightarrow$ cows + are useful
      breathe   + cows $\Rightarrow$ cows + breathe
  In brief, T5 is OBL in English whether N is +def or – def and
whether V1 is +v or – v, but in Arabic it is OBL if V1 is –v.[10]

T6 (OBL):   Ergative-Agent Permutation

This rule forces Erg and Ag to exchange positions to give a neutral
meaning, e.g., *kataba ?al walad risa:lat* "the boy wrote a letter".

SD: X˘V + Erg + Ag + Y
SC: X˘V + Ag + Erg + Y
       $1 + 2 + 3 + 4 \Rightarrow 1 + 3 + 2 + 4$

Condition:
  (1) The meaning is wanted to be neutral.
  (2) and the absence of the case that Erg is –sep and Ag is +sep.

Example: qaTa9a + ħabl   + sami:r + bi hi[11]
            $\Rightarrow$ qaTa9a + sami:r + ħabl   + bi hi

Application: S2, S5, S27 in the corpus.

Discussion:
  (1) Y is put in the SD to cover the probability of having Inst, Loc,
      or adverbial time there. However, Y may be zero.
  (2) If the meaning is wanted to be coloured, i.e., non-neutral, Erg
      may remain before Ag: qaTa9a + ħabl + sami:r. This unusual
      order functions as an unfamiliar stimulus which attracts attention
      to the statement.
  (3) If Erg is – sep and Ag is + sep, Erg must remain before Ag:
      qaTa9a + hu + sami:r

---

[10] Most conclusions in this work are the outcome of tedious drafting, which is not
shown here for the purposes of economy, clarity, and readability.
   [11] *bi hi* = "with it"

(4) If both are – sep. T6 is to be applied:

qaTa9a + hu + tu $\Rightarrow$ qaTa9a + tu + hu[12]

Comparison: There is no such a T-rule in English.

T7 (OPT): *Ergative Deletion*

This rule optionally deletes Erg if it is understood by both sender and receiver of the sentence. Such a rule is needed to account for such sentences as *šariba ?al waladu* or *?akal ?al waldu*.

SD: X^V + Erg + Ag
SC: X^V + Ø + Ag
1 + 2 + 3 + 4 $\Rightarrow$ 1 + Ø + Ag

Condition: Erg is understood and V is + transitive.

Example: šariba + am:? + ?al walad "the boy drank water".
$\Rightarrow$ šariba + Ø + ?al walad "the boy drank".

Application: S8, S13, S14, S15, S28, S40, S52.

Discussion: One may argue against this deletion by saying if Erg is to be deleted it should not be there in the first place. But this can be easily justified by saying that Erg is there and then is deleted. The arguments for this are more than one, Firstly, there are instances where Erg is not deleted, e.g., *šariba ?al walad ma:?*, and there are cases where it is, e.g., *šariba ?al walad*. What other than Erg deletion can better explain the relation between these two sentences? Secondly, if the receiver of the message cannot understand the sentence well he usually asks *šariba ma:ða* "drank what". This proves that the Erg is there but it is deleted optionally.

Comparison: A similar deletion is allowed in English: John drinks + wine $\Rightarrow$ John drinks + Ø. Of course, deleting Erg, in this case the object, depends on V situation. The whole business of optional deletion is due to the tendency of a language to economize wherever possible.

---

[12] This means "I cut it", where "I" means *tu* and "it" means *hu*.

T8 (OPT):   *Instrument-Agent Permutation*

This rule switches Inst and Ag over optionally. The base supplies Inst-Ag order, which is not the normal or neutral order in Arabic, where Ag tends to precede Inst, e.g., *kataba ?al walad bi ?al qalam.*

SD: $X^{\wedge}V$ + Inst + Ag
SC: $X^{\wedge}V$ + Ag + Inst
          $1 + 2 + 3 \Rightarrow 1 + 3 + 2$

Condition: There is no external condition.

Example: kataba + bi ?al qalam + ?al walad
          $\Rightarrow$ kataba +   ?al walad   + bi ?al qalam

Application: S13.

Discussion: The familiar order is Ag then Inst, e.g., *kataba ?al walad bi ?al qalam.* However, any novelty in order, i.e., divergence from the normal, adds strength to the stimulus, using the terms of psychology: *kataba bi ?al qalam ?al walad.* In fact, if the sentence is to be neutral, this rule should be OBL and not optional.

Comparison: There is no such rule in English.

T9 (OBL):   *Locative Copying*

This rule puts a copy of Loc in front of the sentence when the noun of Erg is not definite because a nondefinite noun is not usually allowed to stand initially in Arabic. Such a rule is needed to account for such a sentence as *huna: kita:b 9ala ?al Ta:wilat.*

SD: Erg + Loc[13]
SC: Loc + Erg + Loc
          $1 + 2 \Rightarrow 2 + 1 + 2$

Condition: N of Erg is – def.

Example: kita:b + 9ala ?al Ta:wilat
          $\Rightarrow$ *9ala ?al Ta:wilat + kita:b + 9ala ?al Ta:wilat
          The output is intermediate and must be followed by other T-rules.

---

[13] This SD is the output of T3 (*yaku:n* Deletion) and other T-rules.

Application: S16.

Discussion: If N of Erg is definite, this rule is no more obligatory; it becomes optional: *9ala ?al Ta:wilat ?al kita:b* and *?al kita:b 9ala ?al Ta:wilat* are both acceptable. It seems that there is a general tendency in languages not to begin with the unknown, which highly corresponds to the nondefinite. This seems also to explain why Arabic does not usually allow beginning a sentence with a nondefinite.

Comparison: This rule is applied to similar English sentences but optionally when N of Erg is – def: is a book + on the table
$\Rightarrow$ *on the table + is a book + on the table.

T10 (OBL):   Locative Pronominalization[14]

This rule must follow T9 to put a pronominalized Loc in the place of the first Loc. It is needed to make the output of the previous T-rule (T9) grammatical because *9ala ?al Ta:wilat kita:b 9ala ?al Ta:wilat* is not grammatical.

SD: Loc + Erg⌢Loc
      This is exactly the output of T9.
SC: ProLoc + Erg⌢Loc +
      1 + 2 $\Rightarrow$ ProLoc + 2

Condition: This rule must follow T9.

Example: 9ala ?al Ta:wila + kita:b 9ala ?al Ta:wilat
      $\Rightarrow$ huna: + kita:b 9ala ?al Ta:wilat
      The word *huna:ka* may be used instead of *huna*.

Application: S1, S16.

Discussion: The argument for this explanation is that *9ala ?al Ta:wilat* is Loc or an adverb of place and *huna:ka* is an adverb of place though it is here an adverbial remnant. Further, the fact that both *huna:* and *huna:ka* can take that slot proves that the slot was originally occupied by a locative phrase.

---

[14] Fillmore uses the terms "left-copy" and "right-copy", but these terms are avoided here because "right and left" depend on writing direction.

Comparison: There is a similar T-rule in English:
   on the table + is a book + on the table
   $\Rightarrow$ there   + is a book + on the table.
   The word "is" appears because English does not have a copula deletion rule that corresponds to *yaku:n* deletion.

T11 (OBL):   *Ergative-Locative permutation*

This rule forces Erg and Loc to exchange positions if N of Erg is – def because it is not usually permissible to begin a sentence with a nondefinite noun. The PS-rules supply such a sentence as *kita:b 9ala ?al Ta:wilat*, but this structure must be transformed to a grammatical one.

SD: Erg + Loc
SC: Loc + Erg
       $1 + 2 \Rightarrow 2 + 1$

Condition: N of Erg is – def.

Example: kita:b + 9ala ?al Ta:wilat
       $\Rightarrow$ 9ala ?al Ta:wilat + kita:b

Application: S16.

Discussion: This rule is applied as an alternative to T9. This is why the SD of T9 is the same as the SD of T11. Both rules want to avoid beginning the sentence with a nondefinite noun. If T9 is applied to this SD, T11 cannot nor need be applied.
   However, if N of Erg is + def, T11 becomes optional:
       ?al kita:b + 9ala ?al Ta:wilat
   $\Rightarrow$ 9ala ?al Ta:wilat + ?al kita:b

Comparison: This rule is rarely applied in English though it is common in Arabic. This explains why some Arab learners equate a common Arabic pattern into a rare English one by writing such a sentences as "in the room is a man", a correct sentence but for a wrong reason.

T12 (OPT):   *Passive Transformation*

This rule changes the active verb into a passive verb regardless of the transitivity or intransitivity of the verb and allows the deletion of the agent (Ag), e.g., *kutibat risa:latun* "a letter was written".

SD: V + X⌒N + Ag
SC: Vp + X⌒N + (Ag)
        1 + 2 + 3 ⟹ 1p + 2 + (3)
        where Vp means the passive form of the verb, e.g., *kutiba* or *futiħa*.

Condition: As SD tells, there should be two N's at least and one of them is Ag. The V need not be + transitive.

Example: kataba + risa:lat + min ?al walad
        ⟹   *kutiba + risa:lat + (min ?al walad)
            This is an intermediate structure, which needs further T-rules.

Application: S29.

Discussion: The Vpassive (Vp) is to be supplied by morphophonemic rules (M-rules), e.g., kataba + p → kutiba. The parenthesis round Ag in SC suggests that the Ag may be kept or deleted. The preposition in Ag is not deleted because it is needed and because Ag is not made a subject here. The N is SD may be dominated by Loc, Inst, Dat, of Erg; these are respective examples: kutiba 9ala /al Ta:wilat "the table was written at". kutiba bi ?al qalam "the pen was written with". ?u9Tiya ?al walad kita:b "the boy was given a book". kutibat ?al risa:lat "the letter was written".

Comparison: There is a similar T-rule in English:
        John ate the apple ⟹ the apple was eaten (by John).
        Both languages make the deletion of Ag optional. In English however, the "be" segment is added before V, whereas no such segment is added in Arabic. This difference may cause a wrong generalization by Arab students: the book written.

T13 (OBL):   Verbal Agreement

This rule puts V1 in gender and person agreement with the surface subject, which may be Loc, Inst, Ag, Erg, or Dat. This rule is obligatory in all sentences of the language because every sentence has a verbal and at least one noun; the verbal must agree with that surface subject to make the sentence grammatical, e.g., *maša ?al walad*. However, the surface subject corresponds to tradition *fa:9il*, which will mislead if literally translated into "doer" because the so-called *fa:9il* may be Inst, e.g., *fataħa ?al mifta:ħ ?al ba:b*.

SD: Aux⌢Vl + N   + X
$$\begin{bmatrix} \mp\text{gender} \\ \mp\text{person} \end{bmatrix}$$

SC: Aux⌢   +   N   + X
$$\begin{bmatrix} \mp\text{gender} \\ \mp\text{person} \end{bmatrix} \qquad \begin{bmatrix} \mp\text{gender} \\ \mp\text{person} \end{bmatrix}$$

where gender is + masc or − masc and person is I, II, or III. The square brackets denote that if N is + mas, Vl should be + masc, if N is + III, Vl should + III, and so on.[15]

Condition: N is the surface subject.

Example: past + kataba + layla: + ?al risa:lat
    ⇒   katabat   + layla: + ?al risa:lat

Application: All sentences in the corpus need this rule.

Discussion:
(1) The varieties of such agreement are supplied by L-rules: present + kataba + [− masc] + III → taktubu.
(2) Number agreement will be taken care of in T14.
(3) The gender features and person features are supplied by L-rules in Chapter V.
(4) This rule applies to all verbals (Vl) whether they are + v or − v; that is why it is called "verbal agreement" and not "verb agreement"
(5) Aux should appear in SD because present or past combines with gender and person to give the final form of the verbal. However, if Aus is ka:na or yaku:n, a similar agreement must be guaranteed as well, which might be called Aux agreement, e.g., ka:na ?al walad huna: and ka:nat ?al bint huna.

Comparison:
(1) In English there is no gender agreement between Vl and subject, e.g., he came and she came.
(2) English shows no person agreement except rarely: I came, you came, they came. The exceptions are verb "to be" and the present third person singular: I am, he is, they are and he comes vs. I come.

---

[15] This SC is not expressed in figures because this will complicate the description or at least will not make it any simpler.

T14 (OPT):   *Noun Copying*

This rule copies N in front of Aux V1 and substitutes a pronoun in the place of the copied N. This rule is needed to account for most sentences that begin with initial N such as *?al ?awla:d katabu*:

SD: Aux⌐V1⌐ X + N
SC: N + Aux⌐V1⌐ X + Pro
        $1 + 2 \Rightarrow 2 + 1 + Pro$
        Where Pro is a pronoun that replaces N and agrees with it in gender, number, person, and case.

Condition: N is + definite.

Example:
   (1)   kataba + ?al ?awla:d
      $\Rightarrow$?al ?awla:d + kataba + u:[16]
   (2)   kataba ?al walad bi + ?al qalam
      $\Rightarrow$?al qalam + kataba ?al walad bi + hi
   (3)   kataba + /al walad
      $\Rightarrow$?al walad + kataba + Ø

Application: S6, S14, S36.

Discussion:
   (1) This rule cannot be condensed with T9 (Loc Copying) because T9 is OBL whereas T14 is OPT and because T9 copied Loc whereas T14 copies N, which may be a part of Loc, e.g.,
        kataba 9ala + ?al Ta:wilat
      $\Rightarrow$?al Ta:wilat + katab 9ala + ha:[17]
   (2) If Aux is imperative, the rule becomes OBL because T19 *(mubtada? Deletion)* must operate.
        (?al walad) + ?uktub + Ø
   (3) If N is not definite, the rule may be applied but it must be followed by T29 (Mubtada? Copying) because Arabic does not generally allow the initial N to be − def.

---

[16] M-rules change *kataba* + u: into *katabu:*
[17] M-rules will produce *9alayha:*

(4) If L-rules say that a certain pronoun is – sep (not separable), that Pro must be attached to the verb if Pro is surface subject or object:

?al risa:lat kataba*ha*: ?al walad

(5) If Pro copies the subject, it is zero in certain cases which are supplied by M-rules:

1st person + present, e.g., *?aktubu, naktubu*

3rd person + sing, e.g., *kataba, katabat, taktubu, yaktubu*

2nd person + masc + sing + non past, e.g., *taktubu, ?uktub*

However, if the separable equivalent of these pronouns is originally there, T14 becomes OBL, e.g.,

yaktub	min	huwa
⇒ yaktub	Ø	huwa
⇒ huwa yaktub	Ø	Ø

(6) If Pro stands for a subject, it is always inseparable, e.g., ?al ?awla:d katab*u*:.

(7) If Pro stands for an object, it is usually inseparable and must be attached to the verb, e.g., ?al risa:latu katabaha:. However, if Pro is separable, it must be fronted and the original copied object must be deleted, e.g., *?iyya:ha kataba*.

Comparison: There is no such T-rule in English.

T15:   *Void*

This rule is now void. There was a rule here called Pro-deletion, which was designed to delete some pronouns such as *huwa* in *kataba huwa*. But it was thought that a zero pronoun in the previous rule can solve the problem better. As a result, T15 was cancelled, but the number is retained for the sake of consistent reference to rule numbers and to show the kind of revision procedures needed in such a grammar.

T16 (OBL):   *Case Introduction*

This rule is needed to supply every noun with the proper case ending depending on its position. This is usually applied finally: when N takes its final position.

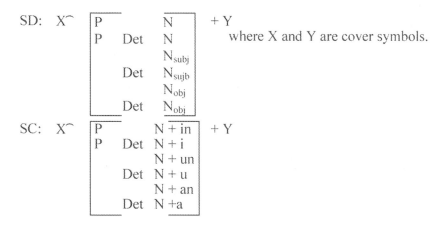

SD: X^

SC: X^

Condition: It is applied when the position of N is settled because this implies economy in the rule usage and because case endings are surface syntactic markers.

Example: kataba + sami:r + + risa:lat   + 9ala ?al Ta:wilat
   ⇒   kataba +sami:r*un* + risa:lat*an* + 9ala ?al Ta:wilat*i*

Application: It must be applied to all sentences in the corpus that contain nouns.   If the noun of the sentence is deleted, this rule cannot be applied, e.g., *kataba*.

Discussion:
   (1) Numbers are not used in SC to avoid complexity.
   (2) [ ] [ ] mean parallel transformation.
   (3) Subject here stands for traditional *mubtada?* and traditional surface *fa:9il*.
   (4) This rule does not account for foreign nouns, duals and regular plurals.

Comparison: This rule is not needed in English, which is an uninflected language.   The inflectional morpheme only shows itself in a few pronouns: I, me, he, him, she, her, we, us, they, whom, whose.

T17 (OBL):   *Reflexive Transformation*

   This rule is needed to change the second NP into a reflexive pronoun if it is a repetition of the same NP in the same sentence.   This implies that the verb is transitive.

SD: $X^\frown V + Y^\frown NP_1^\frown Z + NP_2$
SC: $X^\frown V + Y^\frown NP_1^\frown Z + Ref$
        $1 + 2 + 3 \Rightarrow 1 + 2 + Ref$
        where Ref = reflexive pronoun, e.g., *nafsahu*.

Condition:
   (1) NP_1 and NP_2 are co-referential, i.e., refer to the same referent.
   (2) the same referent.
   (2) V is +tr.

Example: ra?a + ?al waladu + ?al walada
             $\Rightarrow$ ra?a: + ?al waladu + nafsahu

Application: S12

Discussion:
   (1) The SD can be put differently as this:
         $X^\frown V^\frown N_{Ag} + N_{Erg}$
   (2) This reflexive *nafsahu* is different from the emphatic *nafsahu*.
   (3) Ref stands for the whole nominal phrase and not for N only.
   (4) Ref has to agree in gender, numbers and person with NP_2, which
       is there partly for this reason.

Comparison: There is a similar obligatory T-rule in English:
      The boy saw + the boy
   $\Rightarrow$ the boy saw + himself

T18:   *Determiner Transformation*

This rule is needed to move Det that precedes N to a position that directly follows N when Det is not *?al*, e.g., *kitab:bu ?al waladi*.

SD: $(X) + Det + N + Y$
        where X and Y are cover symbols that may be there.
SC: $(X) + N + Det_{gen} + (Y)$
        $(1) + 2 + 3 + (4) \Rightarrow (1) + 3 + 2_{gen} + (4)$

Condition: Det is not *?al*

Example: ?al bayt + busta:n + kabi:r
            $\Rightarrow$ busta:n + ?al bayti + kabi:r
Application: S18, S34, S45.

Discussion:
   (1) The argument for taking *?al bayt* as Det were mentioned in
       Section V.4. Other solutions such as *?al busta:n yaku:n li ?al bayt*

or *?al busta:n yaxuS ?al bayt* are found to be less simple than this Det solution of T18.

(2) The other within Det N is supplied by PS-rules

Comparison: English does not need such a rule in its previous form:
   (1) Whether Det is "the" or N, it remains before N, e.g., the book the boy's book, his book.
   (2) If P remains in Det, then Det must be moved after N:
      of the boy + the book $\Rightarrow$ the book + of the boy.

T19 (OPT):   mubtada? Deletion

This rule optionally deleted (Det) N when it is *mubtada?*, i.e., at the beginning of S, after applying T14 (Noun Copying). This is needed to account for a sentence like *katabu.*:

SD: N + Aux⌢V⌢X + Pro
SC: Ø + Aux⌢V⌢X + Pro
     1 + 2 + 3 $\Rightarrow$ Ø + 2 + 3

Condition: This is applied after T14, because *mubtada?* cannot be deleted unless there is a pro-copy of it, which is supplied by T14.

Example: ?al ?awla:du + katab + u:
   $\Rightarrow$ Ø   + katab + u:

Application: S19, S51.

Discussion: If the sentence is imperative, this rule becomes OBL:
     ?al walad + ?uktub + Ø
 $\Rightarrow$ Ø   + ?uktub + Ø

Comparison: This rule is not used in English except when the sentence is imperative:
    You + write $\Rightarrow$ Ø + write.
In contrast with Arabic, in English there is no copy of the deleted subject:
?antum + ?uktub + u: $\Rightarrow$ Ø + ?uktub + u:

T20:   Void

This rule is now void. There was a rule here called "embedded sentence transformation". But it was thought that it is simpler if PS-rules of Fillmore are modified in a way that makes such T-rule unnecessary. The original order in PS5 of Fillmore's base is:

NP → P (Det) (S) (N).

This is modified into NP → P (Det) N (S) because in Arabic the modifying S follows N.

However, the number T20 is retained because the whole work keeps referring to T-rules in their original numbers, i.e., numbers that they had before cancelling T20.

T21 (OPT): *Special Verb Transformation*

This rule allows the deletion or substitution of some transitive verbs such as those of temptation, warning, and exception and usually keeps the object in the accusative as a mark of that verb deletion.

SD:
| ?ilzam |
| ?ihðar |
| S + ?astaθni |
| V⌢Y⌢wa + ħa:ða: |
| yuna:da |
+ X⌢N

SC:
| Ø |
| (iyya:ka wa) |
| S + ?illa: |
| V⌢Y⌢wa + Ø |
| (ya:) |
+ X⌢N

Condition: This rule must be applied after T16 (Case Introduction), because if the verb is deleted it will be difficult to determine the cases of nouns in the surface structure.

Example:

(1) ?ilzam + ?al bayta ⇒ Ø + ?al bayta[18]

(2) ?ihðar + /al na:ra ⇒ (?iyya:ka wa) + ?al na:ra

(3) kataba ?al ?awla:du + ?astaθni: + sami:ran
⇒ kataba ?al ?awla:du + ?illa: + sami:ran

(4) sa:ra sami:run wa + ħa:ða: + ?al nahra
⇒ sa:ra sami:run wa + Ø + ?al nahra

---

[18] *?ilzam* "stick to" is for traditional *?igra:?* "temptation" *?ihðar* "beware" is for traditional *tahði:r* "warning". *?astaθni:* "I except" is for traditional *?istiθna:?* "exception". *ħa:ða:* "went along" is for *maf9u:l ma9ahu* "accompaniment object". *yuna:da:* "is called" is for *nida:?* "addressing".

(5) yuna:da + sami:run ⇒ (ya:) + sami:ru

Application: S37, S38, S40, S22

Discussion: xx
  (1) This rule deals with a variety of structures which have a verb as a common element. This verb is deleted in four cases and substituted in one case, i.e., *?illa*.
  (2) No numbers are assigned for the SC because the rule is not highly formal.
  (3) This rule deals with some verbs and does not apply to any verbal that is not a verb. That is why it is called as it is.
  (4) Square brackets are used to indicate parallel transformations.
  (5) N keeps the same case ending except for a minor change with yuna:da:, where *un* becomes *u*.
  (6) *?ilzam* and *?iħðar* must be imperative here. *?ataθni:* and *yuna:da:* must be non-impertive. *ħa:ða:* must be in accordance with the preceding V whether the latter is imperative or not   If these conditions are not satisfied, the verb cannot be deleted.
  (7) M-rules are needed to change some outputs such as wa + ?al + nahara → wannahra

Comparison: V-deletion is rare in Arabic and English as well because the verb is so important that it seriously affects meaning to delete it. However, both languages allow V-deletion in a few cases.
  (1) English has a similar "beware" transformation:
      beware + the fire ⇒ ∅ + the fire
  (2) English has a similar "exception" transformation:
      all the boys sat + I except + John
      ⇒ all the boys sat + but + John
  (3) English has a similar "addressing" transformations:
      is addressed + John ⇒ (oh) + John, where "oh" is optional
  (4) However, English does not have "temptation" or "accompaniment" transformations, i.e., *?ilzam* and *ħa:ða:* equivalents.

T22 (OBL):   *Relative Transformation*

This T-rule embeds a sentence into another using a relative pronoun such as *?allaði:* or *?allati:* provided there is a common N in the two sentences.

SD: X⌢N + [Ń + Y]s
       where Ś is the embedded sentence.

SC: X⌢N + Rel + Y
      1 + 2 + 3 ⇒ 1 + Rel + 3

Condition:
    (1) N and Ń are identical and definite.
    (2) This rule must be applied after T14 (Noun Copying), which
        produces that order of Ś.

Example: ?inqaTa9a ?al ħablu + ?al ħablu + ?ištaraytuhu
       ⇒ ?inqaTa9a ?al ħablu + ?llaði: + ?ištaraytu(hu)

Application: S46.

Discussion:
    (1) This rule is not a generalized nor optional rule. The SD comes from
        the PS-rules, where NP → P (Det) N (S).
    (2) Being a pronoun, the relative agrees with N in gender, number,
        and case. Such features are provided by L-rules.
    (3) As the conditions tell, if N is − def no relative can be supplied.
        In this case, the second sentence is merely put after the common N
        in the first sentence: *?inaqTa9a ħablun + ?ištaraytuhu* provided
        that the second N is pronominalized. In other words, Rel here is
        Ø.

Comparison: There is a similar T-rule in English though different
    processes are needed:
      the boy I saw the boy came.
  ⇒ the boy whom I saw came.
    (1) In English, the relative and the pronoun cannot exist together in
        Ś whereas in Arabic they may . However, the object pronoun in
        Ś may be deleted in Arabic:
        ?inqaTa9a ?al ħablu ?allaði: ?ištaraytu(hu)
    (2) The English accusative relative may be deleted, but not the
        Arabic one:
        the boy (whom) I saw came.
    (3) English distinguishes between restrictive and non-restrictive
        clauses structurally and phonologically but Arabic distinguishes
        between them phonologically only:
        wa:lidi: ?allaði: huwa fi: 9amma:n mari: D.
        "My father, who is in Amman, is sick".
        In English non-restrictive clauses, "that" cannot be used and no
        relative can be deleted and commas have to be supplied. In
        Arabic, nothing is done to mark non-restriction except for a
        sustained juncture.

T23 (OPT):   *Emphatic Transformation*

This rule shows how emphasis and insistence are introduced. Emphasis deals with a verb or a noun, whereas insistence deals with the truth value of the whole sentence.

SD: Emph + $\begin{bmatrix} X^\frown V \\ X^\frown N \\ [N^\frown X]_s \end{bmatrix}$

        where Emph is supplied by the base modality.

SC: $\left\{ \begin{matrix} ?inna \\ S \end{matrix} \right\}$ $+ \begin{bmatrix} X^\frown V & + \left\{ \begin{matrix} N_{abstract\ acc} \\ V \end{matrix} \right\} \\ X^\frown N & + \left\{ \begin{matrix} nafs \\ N \end{matrix} \right\} \\ N_{acc}X \end{bmatrix}$

Condition:
    (1) The abstract N after V is made accusative.
    (2) *nafs* must be after N that is +def.
    (3) N after *?inna* is made accusative.

Example:
    (1)   Emph + ?al walad *maša:*
           $\Rightarrow$?al walad maša: + mašyan
      or $\Rightarrow$?al walad maša: maš:
    (2)   Emph + maša *?al waladu*
            maša: ?al waladu + nafsuhu
      or $\Rightarrow$ maša: ?al waladu + ?al waladu
    (3)   Emph sami:run ka:tibun darsahu
           $\Rightarrow$?inna + sami:run ka:tibun darsahu
      or $\Rightarrow$ sami:run katibun darsahu + sami:run ka:tibun darsahu

Application: S33, S34, S43.

Discussion:
    (1) The first tow sub-rules involve contrastive emphasis of a verb and then of a noun, but the third sub-rule involves insistence on the truth value of the whole sentence.
    (2) N that emphasizes a previous N should be identical with it in form and case ending.

(3) *nafs* must be identical in case to the emphasized N and must carry a genitive inseparable pronoun that refers to the emphasized N.

Comparison:
   (1) As for V-emphasis, English rarely uses the cognate object whereas Arabic does that sparely: *maša: mašyan*, but not "he walked walking".
   (2) As for N-emphasis, both languages use the *nafs* "self" forms to emphasize N.
   (3) As for insistence, English does not use a particle like *?inna*, but both use sentence adverbials such as truly, surely, and *ḥaqqan*. However, English uses a method unused in Arabic to insist on the truth of S, e.g., de did come.
   (4) As for repetition as a means of emphasis, both language allow it but more in speech than in writing.

T24 (OPT):   Identical Element Deletion

This rule allows the deletion of the second element when it appears in both simple sentences. The rule is needed to account for conjoined sentences and apposition.

SD: X + Y + wa + X + Z
        where X is the identical element
SC: X + Y + wa + $\emptyset$ + Z
        $1 + 2 + 3 + 4 + 5 \Rightarrow 1 + 2 + 3 + \emptyset + 5$

Condition: If X is a verb and the two N's refer to the same person or thing, the rule becomes OBL and *wa* must be deleted:
   X + Y + $\emptyset$ + $\emptyset$ + Z
   $1 + 2 + 3 + 4 + 5 \Rightarrow 1 + 2 + \emptyset + \emptyset + 5$

Example:
   (1)   maša + sami:run + wa + maša + 9allyyun
        $\Rightarrow$ maša + sami:run + wa + $\emptyset$ + 9allyyun
   (2)   maša + ?al waladu + wa + kataba + ?al waladu
        $\Rightarrow$ maša + ?al waladu + wa + kataba + $\emptyset$
   (3)   maša + ?al waladu + wa + maša: + sami:run
        $\Rightarrow$ maša + ?al waladu + $\emptyset$ + $\emptyset$ + sami:run

Application: S10, S44

Discussion:

(1) This rule accounts for verb deletion, noun deletion, conjunctional sentences, and apposition. Thus it does the function of several rules.

(2) The first example is V-deletion, the second is N-deletion, and the third is apposition, where *sami:r* and *?al walad* are co-referential.

Comparison:

(1) English has a similar identical N-deletion:

The boy + came + and + the boy + sat

$\Rightarrow$ The boy + came + and + $\emptyset$ + sat

(2) English has a similar identical V-deletion:

The boy + sat + and + John + sat

$\Rightarrow$ The boy + $\emptyset$ + and + John + sat

Here the two languages differ in which element to delete depending on the structures allowed by each language, e.g., "the boy sat and John" is not allowed.

(3) English has a similar apposition transformation, which can be described in two ways:

The boy + who is + John + came

$\Rightarrow$ The boy + $\emptyset$ + John + came

or The boy + came + and + John + came

$\Rightarrow$ The boy + $\emptyset$ + $\emptyset$ + John + came

However, to derive apposition from the relative clause causes other problems in Arabic because of case endings, which do not show in English.

(4) In both languages, a conjoined sentence is ambiguous. "John and Tom broke the window" may mean that each broke it separately or both did it together.

T25 (OBL): *Complement Transformation*

This rule deletes *šay?* "something or it" when it precedes and is equivalent to S, which is supplied by PS5 in the base.

SD: $V \frown X + \check{s}ay + \begin{bmatrix} V \frown Y \\ N \frown Z \end{bmatrix}$

where S can start with a verb or a noun.

SC: $V \frown X + \emptyset + \begin{bmatrix} ?an \frown V \frown Y \\ ?anna \frown N \frown Z \end{bmatrix}$

$$1 + 2 + 3 \Rightarrow 1 + \emptyset + \begin{Bmatrix} \text{?an} \\ \text{?anna} \end{Bmatrix} 3$$

Condition:

   (1) S is an apposition to *šay?*.

   (2) *?an* puts V in the subjunctive present form.

   (3) *?anna* puts N in the accusative case.

Example:

   (1)   ?ara:da + šay?an + yaktubu darsahu

     ⇒ ?ara:da +   Ø   + ?an yaktuba darsahu

   (2)   fahima + šay?an + ?al waladu kataba

     ⇒ fahima + Ø + ?anna ?al walada kataba

        "he understood that the boy had written".

Application: S27.

Discussion:

   (1)   *šay?* may have any case ending, e.g.,

       surirtu bi + šay??n + huwa ǰa:?a

     ⇒ surirtu bi +   Ø   + ?annahu ǰa:?a

       "I was pleased that he came".

   (2)   If V is past, N-copying must be done to produce a sentence that begins with N, because *?an* goes with present forms of verbs that mean present or future but not past.

Comparison:

   (1)   There is a similar T-rule in English:

       he wanted + it + he would write his lesson

     ⇒ he wanted + Ø + to write his lesson.

       he knew + it + the boy was absent

     ⇒ he knew + Ø + that the boy was absent.

   (2)   *?an* and *?anna* correspond to English "to" and "that", where *?an* and "to" act on verbs and *?anna* and "that" act on sentences beginning with N's.

   (3)   "That" may be deleted in English, but *?anna* may not:

       He knew (that) the boy was absent.

   (4)   The assumption of "it" or *šay?* is provided by the PS5:

       NP → P (Det) N (S)

        T26 (OBL):   *Manner Transformation*

This rule transforms S into an adverb of manner when the two verbs are simultaneous and the two agents are identical.

SD: $V_1 \frown N_1 \frown X + [V_2 + N_2 + (Y)]_\acute{S}$
       where Y is optional, and
              $\acute{S}$ is the embedded sentence.
SC: $V_1 \frown N_1 \frown X + Participle_{accus} + \emptyset + (Y)$
       $1 + 2 + 3 + (4) \Rightarrow 1 + Participle + \emptyset + (4)$

Condition:
  (1) V_1 and V_2 are simultaneous.
  (2) N_1 and N_2 are identical definite agents.

Example: waqafa ?al waladu + Daħika + ?al waladu
       $\Rightarrow$ waqafa ?al waladu + Daħikan + $\emptyset$

Application: S24.

Discussion:
  (A)   This rule does not account for structures where agents are not
        identical. In this case, different SD and SC are needed:
        SD: $S + \acute{S}$
        SC: $S + \begin{Bmatrix} wa \\ waqad \end{Bmatrix} + \acute{S}$

        Examples:
           (1)   waqafa ?al waladu + 9aliyyun ǰa:lisun
               $\Rightarrow$ waqafa ?al waladu + wa + 9aliyyun ǰa:lisun
               where *wa* introduces beginning with a noun.
           (2)   waqafa ?al waladu + kataba 9aliyyun
               $\Rightarrow$ waqafa ?al waladu + waqad + kataba 9aliyyun
               where *waqad* introduces a sentence beginning with a
               past verb.

  (B)   This rule does not account for *ħa:l* which modifies the object,
        e.g., *šaribtu ?al ma:?a Sa:fiyan* "I drank the water when it was
        pure."
  (C)   The participle is put in the accusative and it may be an active
        participle or a passive one.

Comparison:
  (1)   The English ly-adverb corresponds to the Arabic participle, e.g.,
        He stood up cheerfully.
        waqafa Da:ħikan
  (2)   The English while-past continuous clause corresponds to *wa*-
        nominal S:

The boy stood up while Ali was sitting.

waqafa ?al waladu wa 9aliyyun ja:lisun.

(3) The English time-past perfect clause corresponds to *waqad*-past verb S:

The boy stood up after Ali had written.

waqafa ?al waladu waqad kataba 9aliyyun.

T27 (OBL):   *Purpose Transformation*

This rule transforms the verb of Ś into an accusative abstract noun if Ś is the purpose of S and the two N's are identical.

SD: $V_1\frown N_1\frown(X) + [V_2 + N_2 + (NP)]_{\acute{s}}\frown$Purpose

where V_1 and N_1 belong to the first sentence and V_2 and N_2 belong to the second

SC: $V_1\frown N_1\frown(X)$ + Abstract$_{accus}$ + Ø + (NP)

$1 + 2 + 3 + 4 \Rightarrow 1 +$ Abstract $+$ Ø $+ 4$

Condition:

(1) N_1 and N_2 are identical agents.

(2) V_2 is purpose of V_1.

Example: waqafa ?al waladu + ?ihtarama + ?al waladu + li ?al muqallimi

  ⇒ waqfa ?al waladu + ?ihtira:man +   Ø   + li ?al mu9allimi

Application: S24.

Discussion:

(1) X and NP in SD are optional.

(2) NP is put to allow for the appearance of P which is needed when the verb is nominalized.

(3) Purpose may come from "Modality" in the base.

Comparison: English shows a similar behavior to express the same semantic relationship:

he stood up + he + respected + the teacher

  ⇒ he stood up + Ø + out of respect + for the teacher

(1) The two languages delete the second agent.

(2) The abstract noun is used in both, but without P before it in Arabic.

(3) Both languages use P before Erg and after the nominalized verb, i.e., the abstract: *li* and "for".

T28 (OBL): *Adjective Transformation*

This rule derives the adjective word from S by deleting N and putting Adj in agreement with N of S in the matters of definiteness ($\mp$def), number, and case.

SD: $X \hat{\ } N \begin{bmatrix} + \text{def} \\ - \text{def} \end{bmatrix} + [\acute{N} + V1 \, {}_{-v}]_{\acute{s}}$

where N and $\acute{N}$ are identical in form, but not necessarily in case. $X \hat{\ } N$ is the matrix S.

SC: $X \hat{\ } N + \emptyset + \begin{bmatrix} ?al \\ \emptyset \end{bmatrix} + V1 {}_{-v}$

$1 + 2 + 3 \implies 1 + \emptyset + \begin{bmatrix} ?al \\ \emptyset \end{bmatrix} + 3$

Condition:
(1) This rule must be applied after T5 (Erg Fronting), which produces the SD.
(2) The adjective must agree with N is $\mp$ def, number, and case.

Example:
(1)   fataḥa ?al mifta:ḥu ?al ba:ba + ?al ba:bu + ?aḥmaru
    $\Rightarrow$ fataḥa ?al mifta:ḥu ?al ba:ba + $\emptyset$ + ?al + ?aḥmara
(2)   fataḥa ?al mifta:ḥub-a:ban + ba:bun + ?aḥmaru
    $\Rightarrow$ fataḥa ?al mifta:ḥu ba:ban + $\emptyset$ + $\emptyset$ + ?aḥmara

Application: S42.

Discussion:
(1) The Adj-N agreement in gender and person is secured by T13 (Verbal Agreement) and, therefore, excluded from this rule.
(2) The SC says if N and $\acute{N}$ are   + def, *?al* is added before V1 to make it +def as well . It also says if N and $\acute{N}$ are   – def, nothing is added before V1 so as to keep it – def.

Comparison: There is an Adj transformation in English, but it is applied differently:
            he opened the door + the door + is + red
    $\Rightarrow$ he opened the door + $\emptyset$ + $\emptyset$ + red
    $\Rightarrow$ he opened the red door.

(1) In both languages, N of Ś, which is identical with N, is deleted.
(2) "is" is deleted because of this Adj T-rule, whereas *yaku:n* is deleted anyhow.
(3) "red" has no case ending, whereas ?aħmar has a case ending. As a result, there is no Adj-N case agreement in English, but there is N-Adj case agreement in Arabic.
(4) In English there is no Adj-N agreement in gender, number, ∓ definiteness, but in Arabic there is N-Adj agreement in these variables.

T29 (OBL):   *mubtada? Copying*

This rule puts a pronoun copy before a *mubtada?* that is − def, because Arabic does not usually allow − def N to begin a sentence:

SD: $N + V1_{-v}$
       which is the output of T5 (Erg or Ag Fronting)
SC: $Pro + N + V1_{-v}$
       $1 + 2 \Rightarrow Pro + 1 + 2$

Condition: N is − def.

Example: bintun + ǰami:latun ⇒ hiya + bintun + ǰami:latun

Application: This rule is applied whenever SD appears.

Discussion:
(1) Pro has to agree with N completely: gender, number, person, and nominative case.
(2) If N in SD appears as N_{-def}, the condition will not be needed.
(3) If N is + hum, it may be I, II, or III, depending on the situation. If N is − hum, it is always III.
(4) T29 cannot be combined with T14 (Noun Copying) because T14 is OPT and T29 is OBL. Further, T14 deals with V1, but T29 deals with $V1_{-v}$. Finally T14 fronts N and adds Pro in its place, but T29 adds Pro initially without fronting N.

Comparison: English has a similar T-rule, but with differences:
   a house is large ⇒ it is a large house
(1) The English transformation is OPT but the Arabic one is OBL.
(2) The English N is put finally but the Arabic N is put medially after Pro.
(3) In both languages, Pro is initial and in agreement with N as each language demands.

T30 (OBL):   *Interrogative Transformation*

This rule takes care of how questions are formed. In fact, several rules might be needed to account for a variety of situations.

SD$_1$:   Inter + X + $\begin{bmatrix} \text{NP}_{\text{Loc}} \\ \text{Tadv} \\ \text{(Det) N}_{-\text{hum}} \\ \text{(Det) N}_{+\text{hum}} \end{bmatrix}$ + (Y)

where Inter comes from "Modality" in PS-rules.

SC$_1$: $\begin{bmatrix} \text{?ayna} \\ \text{mata:} \\ \text{ma} \\ \text{man} \end{bmatrix}$ + X + Ø + (Y)

where (Y) is optional in both SD and SC.

1 + 2 + 3 + 4 $\Rightarrow$ Qw + 2 + Ø + 4

SD$_2$:   Inter + S
SC$_2$: $\begin{Bmatrix} \text{?a + S} \\ \text{ma:ða: ħadaθa} \end{Bmatrix}$

SD$_3$:   Inter⌢V + X
SC$_3$: $\begin{Bmatrix} \text{ma:⌢fa9ala} \\ \text{?ala:⌢V} \end{Bmatrix}$ + X

Condition: There is no external condition.

Example:
   (1)   Inter   + kataba + *huna:*
            $\Rightarrow$?ayna + kataba +   Ø
   (2)   Inter + sa:fara + *?amsi*
            $\Rightarrow$ mata + sa:fara +   Ø
   (3)   Inter + ?inqaTa9a + *?al ħablu*
            $\Rightarrow$ ma: + ?inqaTa9a +   Ø
   (4)   Inter + maša: + *?al waladu*
            $\Rightarrow$ man + maša: +   Ø
   (5)   Inter + *maša ?al waladu*
            $\Rightarrow$?a   + maša: ?al waladu
         or
            $\Rightarrow$ ma:ða: ħdaθa
   (6)   Inter *maša:* + ?al waladu
            $\Rightarrow$ ma: fa9ala + ?al waladu

Application: S45, S48, S49.

Discussion:
(1) This rule provides for questioning nouns, verbs, and sentences.
(2) It is OBL.   However, the matter of OBL or OPT depends on the base and SD: what is OBL in a grammar may be OPT in another grammar.
(3) SC_1 puts two processes into one: fronting the questioned element and substituting a question word (QW) for the combination of Inter and the fronted element. the other alternatives would be to substitute and then front or to front and then substitute. However, it seems that this SC is simpler than these alternatives.

Comparison: English has a similar transformation, but it often involves Aux inversion, which is not the case in Arabic.
(1)   Inter + he went   + *there*
         where + did he go +   Ø
(2)   Inter + he travelled   + *yesterday*
    ⇒ when + did he travel +   Ø
(3)   Inter + *the rop*e + was cut
    ⇒ what +   Ø   + was cut
(4)   Inter + *the boy* + went
    ⇒ who +   Ø   + went
(5)   Inter + *he went*
         what happened

    or

    ⇒ did he go
(6)   Inter + he + *went*
    ⇒ what + did he + do

Looking at these examples, one notices that:

(1) In both languages, question words occupy the initial position in S.
(2) In both languages, any content element of the sentence can be questioned: N, V, S, or Time.
(3) In both languages, there are two types of questions: yes-no questions and WH-questions, the answer of which cannot be "yes" or "no".
(4) The main difference is the Aux –inversion in English, which does not exist in Arabic, and, consequently, causes some mistakes made by Arab learners of English.

T31 (OPT):   *Time Transformation*

This rule puts Time Adverbial at the end of the sentence:

SD: Tadv + X
SC: X + Tadv
        $1 + 2 \Rightarrow 2 + 1$

Condition: There is no external condition.

Example: ?amsi + maša: ?al waladu
        $\Rightarrow$ maša: ?al waladu + ?amsi

Application: S44.

Discussion:
  (1) The position of Tadv is SD is supplied by Modality in PS-rules.
  (2) If the sentence has to be neutral, this rule has to be OBL and not OPT. However, if the sentence has to be grammatical regardless of neutrality, then the rule is OPT.

Comparison: English has the same rule:
  (1)   yesterday + he came
        $\Rightarrow$ he came + yesterday
  (2)   last week + he wasn't here
        $\Rightarrow$ he wasn't here + last week

T32 (OBL):   *Separation Transformation*

This rule adds a separation pronoun between the subject (N) and the predicate $V1_{-v}$ if both are + def. This is done in order not to confuse the predicate with the adjective or a sentence with a phrase.

SD: $N_{+def} + ?al^\frown V1_{-v}$
SC: $N + Pro + ?al^\frown V1_{-v}$
        $1 + 2 \Rightarrow 1 + Pro + 2$

Condition: Both N *(mubtada?)* and $V1_{-v}$ *(xabar)* are + def.
    This condition is explicit in SD.

Example: 9umar + /al 9a:dilu
        $\Rightarrow$ 9umar + huwa + ?al 9a:dilu

Application: S25.

Discussion: Without putting Pro in between, one may take *?al 9a:dilu* as an adjective *9umar* and thus the complete sentence would be taken as a fragment of a sentence. To avoid this confusion, Pro is added to break the N-Adj sequence.

Comparison: There is no such rule in English, because the adjective in English does not take Det and, as a result, there is no place for confusion.   Further, the subject and the predicate in English are usually separated by Aux V1, the first of which may be deleted such as in the case of *yaku:n* and the second of which may not be there to start with such as in the case of V1 $_{-v}$, e.g., John is just.

T33 (OBL):   Ergative-Instrument Permutation

This rule permutes Erg and Inst if there is no Agent. This permutation is OBL to put S in the normal and neutral order.

SD: V $_{+tr}$ + Erg + Inst
SC: V $_{+tr}$ + Inst + Erg
        $1 + 2 + 3 \Rightarrow 1 + 3 + 2$

Condition: As SD tells, V is transitive and there is no Ag.

Example: fataha + li ?al ba:b + bi ?al mifta:h
        $\Rightarrow$ fataha + ?al mifta:hu + ?al ba:ba
        where *bi* is deleted because of T1 (Subj P Del), *li* of Erg is deleted by T2 (Obj P Del), and cases are supplied by T16 (Case Introduction).

Application: S4.

Discussion:
  (1) This transformation is necessary to produce the unmarked, i.e., neutral, order within the sentence.
  (2) If Ag exists, then T6 (Erg-Ag Permutation) is applied.

Comparison:
  (1)   There is a similar rule in English, but Inst is fronted because V cannot usually start a sentence in English:
        opened the door + with the key
     $\Rightarrow$ The key + opened the door
  (2)   however, Erg-Inst permutation is applied in English if what is operated on is this SD:
        the door + was opened + with the key

$\Rightarrow$ the key + opened + the door
where the passive verb is changed into an active one.

(3)   In both languages, this transformation cannot be applied unless Ag is not there, because Ag usually has the priority over Inst in permutation or fronting.

T34 (OBL):   *Condition Transformation*

This rule introduces a condition particle to two sentences one of which implies the other.

SD: Condition + $[V_1{}^\frown X]_{S_1} + [V_2{}^\frown Y]_{S_2}$

SC: ?in   + $V_1{}^\frown X + V_2{}^\frown Y$
       Condition + 1 + 2 $\Rightarrow$?in + 1 + 2

Condition: V_1 and V_2 are present in form.

Example: Condition + tadrusu + tanjahu
       $\Rightarrow$?in   + tadrus + tanjah

Application: S52

Discussion:
   (1) This rule does not account for all forms of conditional sentences which use a wide variety of condition particles or elements.
   (2) *?in* puts the two verbs, i.e., V_1 and V_2, in the jussive.

Comparison: English has a similar T-rule:
   (1)   Condition + you study + you pass
       $\Rightarrow$ if   + you study + you pass
   (2)   Condition + you will study + you will pass
       $\Rightarrow$ if   + you Ø   study + you will pass
   (3)   Condition + sawfa tadrusu + sawfa tanjahu
       $\Rightarrow$ if   +   Ø tadrus   + fa sawfa tanjahu

Comparing the two languages, one notices that:
   (1) Both languages do not allow future markers in the conditional clause: both "will" and *safwa* are deleted in the previous examples.
   (2) *?in* affects the ends of the two verbs by putting them in the jussive, but "if" does not.
   (3) *?in* is usually followed by a verb, but "if" is usually followed by N.

(4) Both languages allow the conditional clause to precede or follow the main clause.

T35 (OPT): Instrument or Locative Fronting

This rule allows the fronting of Instrument or Locative:

SD: $X + \begin{Bmatrix} Inst \\ Loc \end{Bmatrix}$

SC: $\begin{Bmatrix} Inst \\ Loc \end{Bmatrix} + X$

$1 + 2 \Rightarrow 2 + 1$

Condition: There is no external condition.

Example:
  (1)   kataba ?al waladu + bi ?al qalami
      $\Rightarrow$ bi ?al qalami + kataba ?al waladu
  (2)   ?al kita:bu + 9ala ?al Ta:wilati
      $\Rightarrow$ 9ala ?al Ta:wilati + ?al kita:bu

Application: S15.

Discussion:
(1) This rule cannot be combined with T5 (Erg or Ag Fronting), because each needs a different SD and because T5 is OBL and T35 is OPT.
(2) T35 cannot be combined with T14 (Noun Copying) because no Pro takes the place of NP in T35 but Pro replaces the fronted NP in T14. In other words, each SC is different.

Comparison:
(A) English allows such fronting as well:
    (1)   he wrote + with the pen
       $\Rightarrow$ with the pen + he wrote
    (2)   he put the book + on the table
       $\Rightarrow$ on the table + he put the book

(B) These outputs may sound odd because they are out of context; nevertheless, they are grammatical.

(C) This fronting in both languages does not provide the neutral form.   But this form is allowed for special purposes depending on such factors as focus and what is known and not known in the speaker-listener situation.

T36 (OPT):   mawǰu:d Deletion

This rule deletes mawǰu:d "existing" optionally in the presence of Erc Loc whether Aux is ka:na or yaku:nu.

SD: $\begin{Bmatrix} \text{ka : na} \\ \text{yaku : nu} \end{Bmatrix}$ mawǰu:d + Erg Loc

SC: $\begin{Bmatrix} \text{ka : na} \\ \text{yaku : nu} \end{Bmatrix}$ + Ø + Erg Loc

$1 + 2 + 3 \Rightarrow 1 + Ø + 3$

Condition: No external one.

Example: ka:na + mawǰu:d + ?al kita:bu 9ala ?al Ta:wilati

$\Rightarrow$ ka:na +   Ø   + ?al kita:bu 9ala ?al Ta:wilati

Application: S1, S16, S26, S31, S9.

Discussion:

(1)   As was said in T1, the T-rules are not necessarily presented here in the same sequence necessary for application. However, the ordered sequence of application is adhered to in the next chapter, where the T-rules operate collectively to produce surface structures.

(2)   This rule may be modified to account also for equational sentences by deleting the verb the verb yuTa:biq "equals".

yuTa:biq + sami:r + ?ismuhu

$\Rightarrow$ Ø   + sami:r + ?ismuhu

or

yuTa:biq + ?ismuhu + sami:r

$\Rightarrow$ Ø   + ?ismuhu + sami:r

which logically means if A = B, then B = A.

(3)   however, one may think of another solution to the problem of equational sentences. One can assume that if S contains two NP's with equal function, usually Erg, then V1 is zero. This zero V1 finds support in the argument that if no NP has a relation to the other NP other than equivalence, then

no verbal is needed to mark Ag-Erg, Ag-Inst, NP Loc, Ag-Dat, or Erg-Inst relationships.

Comparison: Theoretically, English has a similar rule though the deletion of "existing" is OBL:

the book is + existing + on the table

⇒ the book is +   Ø   + on the table.

CHAPTER SEVEN

TESTING THE GRAMMAR EFFICIENCY

After formulating the necessary T-rules in the previous chapter, one may start applying them to see how surface structures can be produced from deep structures provided by the base, i.e., the PS-rules.

In this chapter, there will be a quick application of T-rules to see how each sentence in the corpus is produced. Of course, each sentence is the outcome of several transformations applied one after the other. This application will show how efficient the grammar is in accounting for such a wide variety of sentences as those of the corpus. In other words, this application will evaluate the total efficiency of the T-rules.

1. S $\longrightarrow$ Aux Vl [P Det N]$_{Erg}$ [P Det N]$_{Loc}$

   $\longrightarrow$ yaku:n mawǰud li ?al kita:b 9ala ?al Ta:wilat

   By T1 (Subject P Deletion):

   $\Longrightarrow$ yaku:n mawǰud Ø ?al kita:b 9ala ?al Ta:wilat

   By T3 (*yaku:n* Del):

   $\Longrightarrow$ Ø mawǰud Ø ?al kita:b 9ala ?al Ta:wilat

   By T36 (*mawǰu:d* Del):

   $\Longrightarrow$ Ø Ø Ø ?al kita:bu 9ala ?al Ta:wilati

   By T16 (Case Introduction):

   $\Longrightarrow$ Ø Ø Ø ?al kita:b 9ala ?al Ta:wilat

   By M-rules:

   $\Longrightarrow$?al kita:bu 9ala TTA:wilati

2. S $\longrightarrow$ Aux Vl [P N]$_{Erg}$ [P N]$_{Da}$ [P Det N]$_{Ag}$

   $\longrightarrow$?a9Ta li kita:b li sami:r min ?al walad

   By T6 (Erg-Ag Perm):

   $\Longrightarrow$?a9Ta min ?al walad li sami:r li kita:b

   By T1 (Subj P Del):

   $\Longrightarrow$?a9Ta Ø ?al walad li sami:r li kita:b

   By T2 (Obj P Del):

   $\Longrightarrow$?a9Ta Ø ?al walad Ø sami:r Ø kita:b

By T13 (Verbal Agreement):

⇒   ?a9Ta Ø ?al   walad   Ø   sami:r   Ø   kita:b

By T16 (Case Introduction):

⇒   ?a9Ta Ø ?al   waladu   Ø   sami:ran   Ø   kita:ban

3. S →   Aux V1   [P Det N]$_{Erg}$

       →   ?inqata9a   li   ?al   ħabl

       By T13 (V1 Agreement):

   ⇒   ?inqata9a   li   ?al   ħabl

       By T2 (Subj P Del):

   ⇒   ?inqata9a   Ø   ?al   ħabl

       By T16 (Case Introduction):

   ⇒   ?inqaTa9a   Ø   ?al   ħabl

       By M-rules

   ⇒   ?inqaTa9a   lħabl

4. S →   Aux V1   [P Det N]$_{Erg}$ [P Det N]$_{Inst}$

       →   fatħa li ?al   ba:b   bi ?al   mifta:ħ

       By T33 (Erg-Inst Penm):

   ⇒   fatħa bi ?al   mifta:ħ   li   ?al   ba:b

       By T1 (Subj P Del);

   ⇒   fatħa Ø ?al   mifta:ħ   li   ?al   ba:b

       By T2 (Obj P Del):

   ⇒   fatħa Ø ?al   mifta:ħ   Ø   ?al   ba:b

       By T13 and T16:

   ⇒   fatħa Ø ?al   mifta:ħu   Ø   ?al   ba:ba

       By M-rules

   ⇒   fatħa lmifta:ħu lba:ba

5. S →   Aux V1   [P N]$_{Erg}$ [P N]$_{Ag}$

       →   qaTa9a li ħabl   min   sami:r

       By T6 (Erg-Ag Perm):

   ⇒   qaTa9a min sami:r   li   ħabl

       By T1 (Subj P Del);

   ⇒   qaTa9a Ø   sami:r   li   ħabl

       By T2 (Obj P Del):

   ⇒   qaTa9a Ø   sami:r   Ø   ħabl

       By T13 (V1 Agr):

$\Rightarrow$ qaTa9a   Ø   sami:r   Ø   ħabl

       By T16 (Case Intr.):

$\Rightarrow$ qaTa9a   Ø   sami:run   Ø   ħablan[1]

6. S $\rightarrow$ Aux V1 [P Det N]$_{Erg}$

   $\rightarrow$ yakburu   li   ?al   walad

       By T1 (Subj P Del):

   $\Rightarrow$ yakburu   Ø   ?al   walad

       By T13 (V1 Agr):

   $\Rightarrow$ yakburu   Ø   ?al   walad

        By T14 (Noun Copying):

   $\Rightarrow$?al   walad   yakburu   Ø Ø

        By T16 (Case Intr.):

   $\Rightarrow$?al   waladu   yakburu   Ø Ø

7. S $\rightarrow$ Aux V1 [P Det N]$_{Ag}$

   $\rightarrow$ yaku:n   Daħu:k   min   ?al walad

       By T1 (Subj P Del):

   $\Rightarrow$ yaku:n   Daħu:k   Ø   ?al walad

       By T3 (*yaku:n* Del):

   $\Rightarrow$ Ø   Daħu:k   Ø   ?al walad

       By T5 (Ag Fronting):

   $\Rightarrow$ Ø   ?al walad   Ø   Daħu:k

       By T13 and T16

   $\Rightarrow$ Ø   ?al waladu   Ø   Daħu:kun

8. S $\rightarrow$ Aux V1 [P N]$_{Erg}$ [P N]$_{Ag}$

   $\rightarrow$ kataba   li   risa:lat   min   sami:r

       By T1 and T2:

   $\Rightarrow$ kataba   Ø   risa:lat   Ø   sami:r

       By T6 (Erg-Ag Perm):

   $\Rightarrow$ kataba   Ø   sami:r   Ø   risa:lat

       By T7 (Erg Del):

   $\Rightarrow$ kataba   Ø   sami:r   Ø   Ø

       By T13 (V1 Agr):

   $\Rightarrow$ kataba   Ø   sami:r   Ø   Ø

       By T16 (Case Intr.):

   $\Rightarrow$ kataba   Ø   sami:run   Ø   Ø

---
[1] No M-rules are needed here.

9. S → Aux V1 [P N]$_{Erg}$ Loc

→ ka:na mawǰu:dan li sami:r huna:
By T1 (Subj P Del):
⇒ ka:na mawǰu:dan Ø sami:r huna:
By T13 (V1 Agr):
⇒ ka:na mawǰu:dan Ø sami:r huna:
By T36 (*mawǰu:d* Del):
⇒ ka:na Ø Ø sami:run huna:

10. S → Aux V1 [P N]$_{Ag}$ wa S → Aux V1 [P Det N]$_{Ag}$

→ maša: min ha:ða wa maša: min ?al walad
By T1 (Subj P Del):
⇒ maša: Ø ha:ða wa maša: Ø ?al walad
By T16 (Case Intr):
⇒ maša: Ø ha:ða wa maša Ø ?al waladu
By T24 (Identical Element Del):
⇒ maša Ø ha:ða Ø Ø Ø ?al waladu
By T13 (V1 Agr):
⇒ maša: Ø ha:ða Ø Ø Ø ?al waladu
By M-Rules:
⇒ maša: ha:ða lwaladu

11. S → Aux V1 [P N]$_{Ag}$

→ maša: min ha:ða
By T1 (Subj P Del):
⇒ maša: Ø ha:ða
By T13 and T16:
⇒ maša: Ø ha:ða

12. S → Aux V1 [P N]$_{Erg}$ [P N]$_{Ag}$

→ ra?a: li ?al walad min ?al walad
By T1 (Subj P Del):
⇒ ra?a: li ?al walad Ø ?al walad
By T2 (Obj P Del):
⇒ ra?a Ø ?al walad Ø ?al walad
By T6 (Erg-Ag Perm):
⇒ ra?a: Ø ?al walad Ø ?al walad
By T17 (Ref T):
⇒ ra?a: Ø ?al walad Ø nafsahu
By T13 and T16:
⇒ ra?a: Ø ?al waladu Ø nafsahu

    By M-rules:
⇒   ra?a: lwaladu nafsahu
13. S   →   Aux Vl [P N]$_{Erg}$ [P Det N]$_{Inst}$ [P Det N]$_{Ag}$
     →   kataba li risa:lat bi ?al qalam min ?al walad
         By T7 (Erg Del):
     ⇒   kataba Ø   bi ?al qalam min ?al walad
         By T1 (Subj P Del):
     ⇒   kataba Ø   bi ?al   qalam   Ø   ?al   walad
         By T13 (Vl Agr):
     ⇒   kataba Ø   bi ?al   qalam   Ø   ?al   walad
         By T16 (Case Intr.):
     ⇒   kataba Ø   bi ?al   qalami Ø   ?al   waladu
         By T8 (Inst-Ag Perm):
     ⇒   kataba Ø   Ø   ?al   waladu   bi   ?al   qalami
         By M-rules:
     ⇒   ?al waladu katab bi lqalami
14. S13   →   kataba ?al   waladu   bi   ?al qalami
               By T14 (N Copying):
          ⇒   ?al   walad   kataba   Ø bi ?al qalami
               By T16 (Case Intr.):
          ⇒   ?al   waladu kataba   Ø bi al   qalami
               By M-rules:
          ⇒   ?al waladu kataba bi lqalami
15. S13   →   kataba ?al wladu bi ?al qalami
               By T35 (Inst Fronting):
          ⇒   bi al qalami kataba   ?al waladu
               By M-rules:
          ⇒   bi lqalami kataba lwaladu
16. S   →   Aux Vl [P Det N]$_{Erg}$ [P Det N]$_{Loc}$
     →   yaku:nu mawǰu:dan li kita:b 9ala: ?al Ta:wilat
         By T3 (*yaku:n* Del):
     ⇒   Ø   mawǰu:dan li kita:b 9ala: ?al Ta:wilat
         By T36 (*mawǰu:d* Del):
     ⇒   Ø   Ø   li kita:b 9ala: ?al Ta:wilat
         By T1 (Subj P Del):
     ⇒   Ø   Ø   Ø kita:b 9ala: ?al Ta:wilat

By T11 (Erg-Loc Perm):

⇒   Ø   Ø   9ala   ?al   Tawilat   Ø   kita:b

By T16 (Case Intr.):

⇒   Ø   Ø   9ala   ?al   Tawilati   Ø   kita:bun

By M-rules

⇒   9ala Tta:wilati kita:bun

17. S   →   Aux   V1   [P Det N]$_{Erg}$

    →   yaku:n   kabi:r   li   ?al   bayt   busta:n

By T3 (*yaku:n* Del):

⇒   Ø   kabi:r   li   ?al   bayt   busta:n

By T1 (Subj P Del):

⇒   Ø   kabi:r   Ø   ?al   bayt   busta:n

By T18 (Det Trans):

⇒   Ø   kabi:r   Ø   busta:n   ?al   bayt

By T13 (V1 Agr):

⇒   Ø   kabi:r   Ø   busta:n   ?al   bayti

By T5 (Erg Fronting):

⇒   Ø   busta:n   ?al   bayti   Ø   kabi:r

By T16 (Case Intr.):

⇒   Ø   busta:n   ?al   bayti   Ø   kabi:run

By M-rules:

⇒   busta:nu lbayti kabi:run

18. S17 →   bustan:nu   ?al   bayti   kabi:run

By T14 (N Copying):

⇒   ?al   bayt   bustan:nu   hu   kabi:run

By T16 (Case Intr.):

⇒   ?al   baytu   bustan:nu   hu   kabi:run

19. S   →   maša: ?al   waladu

By T14 (N Copying):

⇒   ?al   waladu   maša: Ø

By T19 (mubtada? Del):

⇒   Ø   maša: Ø

20. S   →   Neg Aux V1 [P N]$_{Ag}$

    →   ma: maša: min   layla:

By T1 (Subj P Del):

⇒   ma: maša: Ø   layla:

By T13 (V1 Agr):

$\Rightarrow$ ma: maša:t Ø layla:
        By T16 (Case Intr.):
$\Rightarrow$ ma: maša:t Ø layla:

21. S $\rightarrow$ Aux V1 [P Det N]$_{Erg}$

$\rightarrow$ ka:na ǰami:lan li ?al bayt
        By Ta (Subj P Del):

$\Rightarrow$ ka:na ǰami:lan Ø ?al bayt
        By T5 (erg Fronting):

$\Rightarrow$ ka:na Ø   ?al bayt ǰami:lan
        By T16 (Case Intr.):

$\Rightarrow$ ka:na Ø   ?al baytu ǰami:lan
        By T13 (V1 Agr):

$\Rightarrow$ ka:na Ø   ?al baytu ǰami:lan
        By M-rules:

$\Rightarrow$ ka:na lbaytu ǰami:lan

22. S $\rightarrow$ Aux V1 [P N]$_{Ag}$ wa S $\rightarrow$ Aux V1 [P Det N$_{Erg}$[P N]$_{Ag}$

$\rightarrow$ sa:ra min sami:r wa ḥa:ða li ?al nahr min sami:r
        By T1 (Subj P Del):

$\Rightarrow$ sa:ra Ø   sami:r wa ḥa:ða li ?al nahr   Ø   sami:r
        By T2 (Obj P Del):

$\Rightarrow$ sa:ra Ø   sami:r wa ḥa:ða Ø ?al nahr   Ø   sami:r
        By T24 (Id. El. Del):

$\Rightarrow$ sa:ra Ø   sami:r wa ḥa:ða Ø ?al nahr   Ø   Ø
        By T21 (Special V Tr):

$\Rightarrow$ sa:ra Ø   sami:r wa Ø   Ø ?al nahr   Ø   Ø
        By T13 and T16:

$\Rightarrow$ sami:ru   nahr
   sa:ra Ø   n   wa Ø   Ø ?al a   Ø   Ø
        By M-rules:

$\Rightarrow$ sa:ra sami:run wa nnahra

23. S $\rightarrow$ Aux V1 [P N]$_{Ag}$ S $\rightarrow$ Aux V1 [P Det N]$_{Erg}$[P N]$_{Ag}$

$\rightarrow$ waqafa min sami:r ?iḥtarama   li ?al mu9allim
                        min   sami:r
        By T1 (Subj P Del):

$\Rightarrow$ waqafa Ø sami:r ?iḥtarama   li ?al mu9allim
                    Ø   sami:r
        By T27 (Purpose Tr):

$\Rightarrow$ waqafa Ø sami:r ?iḥtara:man li ?al mu9allim
                    Ø   Ø

By T13 and T16

⇒   waqafa   Ø   sami:run   ?iħtara:man   li   ?al   mu9allimi
                              Ø   Ø

By M-rules:

⇒   waqafa sami:run ?iħtara:man li lmu9allimi

24. S   →   Aux V1   [P N]$_{Ag}$ S → Aux V1 [P N]$_{Ag}$

     →   waqafa   min   sami:r   Daħika   min   sami:r
         By T1 (Subj P Del):

     ⇒   waqafa   Ø   sami:r   Daħika   Ø   sami:r
         By T26 (Manner Tr):

     ⇒   waqafa   Ø   sami:r   Daħikan   Ø   Ø
         By T13 and T16:

     ⇒   waqafa   Ø   sami:run   Da:ħikan   Ø   Ø

25. S   →   Aux V1   [P N]$_{Erg}$ [P Det N]$_{Erg}$

     →   yaku:n   Ø   li   9umar   li   ?al   9a:dil
         By T1 (Subj P Del):

     ⇒   yaku:n   Ø   Ø   9umar   Ø   ?al   9a:dil
         By T3 (yaku:n Del):

     ⇒   Ø   Ø   Ø   9umar   Ø   ?al   9a:dil
         By T16 (Case Intr.):

     ⇒   Ø   Ø   Ø   9umaru   Ø   ?al   9a:dilu
         By T32 (Separation Tr)

     ⇒   ?al
         Ø   Ø   Ø   9umaru   huwa   Ø   9a:dilu
         By M-rules:

     ⇒   9umaru huwa l9a:dilu

However, this sentence is partly produced outside Fillmore's base, which fails to account for equational sentences because its Prop does not contain two Ergatives.

26. S   →   Neg Aux V1   [P N]$_{Erg}$ [P Det N]$_{Loc}$

     →   la: yaku:n   mawǰu:d   li   ?aħad   fi: ?al   bayt
         By T3 (yaku:n Del):

     ⇒   la: Ø   mawǰu:d   li   ?aħad   fi: ?al   bayt

         By T36 (mawǰu:d Del):

     ⇒   la: Ø   Ø   li   ?aħad   fi: ?al   bayt
         By T1 (Subj P Del):

     ⇒   la: Ø   Ø   Ø   ?aħad   fi: ?al   bayt
         By T16 (Case Intr.):

     ⇒   la: Ø   Ø   Ø   ?aħada   fi: ?al   bayti

By M-rules:

⇒ la: ?aḥad fi lbayti

27. S → Aux V1 [P N Ś]_{Erg} [P N]_{Ag}

→ ?rui:du li šay? [?aktub risa:lat]_ś min ?ana:
By T1 (Subj P Del):

⇒ ?rui:du li šay? [?aktub risa:lat]_ś Ø ?ana:
By T14 (Noun Copying)

⇒ ?ana ?uri:du li šay? ?aktub risa:lat Ø Ø
By T19 (*mubtada?* Del):

⇒ Ø ?uri:du li šay? ?aktub risa:lat Ø Ø
By T2 (Obj P Del):

⇒ Ø ?uri:du Ø šay? ?aktub risa:lat Ø Ø
By T25 (Compl Tr):

⇒ Ø ?uri:du Ø Ø ?an ?aktuba risal:lat Ø Ø
By T13 and T16

⇒ Ø ?uri:du Ø Ø ?an ?aktuba risal:latan Ø Ø

28. S → Neg Aux V1 [P N]_{Erg} [P Det N]_{Ag}

→ lam yaktub li risa:lat min ?al walad
By T7 (Erg Del):

⇒ lam yaktub Ø min ?al walad
By T1 (Subj P Del):

⇒ lam yaktub Ø Ø ?al walad
By T13 and T16

⇒ lam yaktub Ø Ø ?al waladu
By M-rules:

⇒ lam yaktubi lwaladu

29. S → Aux V1 [P Det N]_{Erg} [P Det N]_{Ag}

→ kataba li ?al risa:lat min ?al walad
By T2 (Obj P Del):

⇒ kataba Ø ?al risa:lat min ?al walad
By T12 (Passiv Tr):

⇒ kutiba Ø ?al risa:lat Ø
By T13 (V1 Agr):

⇒ kutibat Ø ?al risa:lat Ø
By T16 (Case Intr.):

⇒ kutibat Ø ?al risa:latu Ø
By M-rules:

⇒ kutibati rrisa:latu

30. S → Emph Aux V1 [P Det N]$_{Erg}$
   → Emph yaku:n wasi:m   li ?al walada:ni
        By T3 (*yaku:n* Del):
   ⇒ Emph Ø   wasi:m   li ?al walada:ni
        By T1 (Subj P Del):
   ⇒ Emph Ø   wasi:m   Ø ?al walada:ni
        By T13 (V1 Agr):
   ⇒ Emph Ø   wasi:ma:ni   Ø ?al walada:ni
        By T14 (N Copying):
   ⇒ Emph ?al walada:ni Ø wasi:ma:ni Ø
        By T23 (Emph Tr):
   ⇒ ?inna lwaladayni wasi:man:ni

31. Exactly like S26. This is an example of two sentences of the same
    deep structure and the same surface structure: la: walada: fi: ?al
    bayti and la: ?aħada fi: ?al bayti.

32. S → Aux V1 [P Det N]$_{Ag}$
   → ka:da yamši: min   ?al walad
        By T1 (Subj P Del):
   ⇒ ka:da yamši: Ø   ?al walad
        By T14 (N Copying):
   ⇒ ka:da ?al   walad yamši: Ø Ø
        By T13 and T16:
   ⇒ ka:da ?al   waladu yamši:
        By M-rules:
   ⇒ ka:da lwaaladu yamši:

33. S19 →   maša:
    S   →   Emph + maša:
             By T23 (Emph Tr):
        ⇒ maša: mašyan
34. S → Emph Aux V1 [P Det N]$_{Erg}$ [P N]$_{Ag}$
   → Emph yaku:n ka:tib li huwa dars min sami:r
        By T3 (*yaku:n* Del):
   ⇒ Emph Ø   ka:tib li huwa dars min sami:r
        By T1 (Subj P Del):
   ⇒ Emph Ø   ka:tib li huwa dars Ø sami:r
        By T2 (Obj P Del):
   ⇒ Emph Ø   ka:tib Ø huwa dars Ø sami:r

By T5 (Ag Fronting):

⇒ Emph Ø sami:r Ø ka:tib Ø huwa dars

By T18 (Det Tr):

⇒ Emph Ø sami:r Ø ka:tib Ø dars hu

By T23 (Emph Tr):

⇒ ?inna Ø sami:ran Ø ka:tib Ø dars hu

By T13 and T16:

⇒ ?inna Ø sami:ran Ø ka:tibun Ø darsa hu

35. S → Aux V1 [P Det N]$_{Erg}$

→ yaku:n maktu:b li ?al risa:lat

By T3 (*yaku:n* Del):

⇒ Ø maktu:b li ?al risa:lat

By T1 (Subj P Del):

⇒ Ø maktu:b Ø ?al risa:lat

By T13 (V1 Agr):

⇒ Ø maktu:bat Ø ?al risa:lat

By T5 (Erg Fronting):

⇒ Ø ?al risa:lat Ø maktu:bat

By T16 (Case Intr):

⇒ ?al

Ø risa:latu Ø maktu:batun

By M-rules:

⇒ ?arrisa:latu maktu:batun

36. S → Aux V1 [P Det N]$_{Erg}$ [P N]$_{Ag}$

→ ?aǰmala li ?al bayt min ma:

By T1 (Subj P Del):

⇒ ?aǰmala li ?al bayt Ø ma:

By T2 (Obj P Del):

⇒ ?aǰmala Ø ?al bayt Ø ma:

By T14 (N Copying):

⇒ ma: ?aǰmala Ø ?al bayt Ø Ø

By T13 and T16:

⇒ ma: ?aǰmala Ø ?al bayta Ø Ø

By M-rules:

⇒ ma: ?aǰmala lbayta

37. S$_1$ → Aux V1 [P Det N]$_{Erg}$ [P Det N]$_{Ag}$

→ ?ilzam li ?al bayt min ?anta

By T1 (Subj P Del):

⇒ ?ilzam li ?al bayt Ø ?anta

By T2 (Obj P Del):

$\Rightarrow$?ilzam Ø ?al bayt Ø ?anta

By T14 (N Copying):

$\Rightarrow$?anta ?ilzam Ø ?al bayt Ø Ø

By T19 (*mubtada?* Del):

$\Rightarrow$ Ø ?ilzam Ø ?al bayt Ø Ø

By T13 and T16:

$\Rightarrow$ Ø ?ilzam Ø ?al bayta Ø Ø

By T21 (Special V Tr):

$\Rightarrow$ Ø Ø Ø ?al bayta Ø Ø

S_2 $\rightarrow$ Aux V1 [P N]$_{Erg}$ [P N]$_{Ag}$

$\rightarrow$?unadi li sami:r min ?ana

By T12 (Passive Tr):

$\Rightarrow$ yuna:da: li sami:r Ø

By T1 (Subj P Del):

$\Rightarrow$ yuna:da: Ø sami:r Ø

By T16 (Case Intr.):

$\Rightarrow$ yuna:da: Ø sami:run

By T21 (Special V Tr):

$\Rightarrow$ ya: Ø sami:run

38. S $\rightarrow$?iħðar ?al na:ra[2]

By T21 (Special V Tr):

$\Rightarrow$ (?iyyaka
wa) ?al na:ra

By M-rules:

$\Rightarrow$?iyyaka wa nna:ra

39. S $\rightarrow$ Aux V1 [P N]$_{Erg}$ [P N]$_{Ag}$

$\rightarrow$ yaku:n ?aTwal min layla: min sami:r

By T1 (Subj P Del):

$\Rightarrow$ yaku:n ?aTwal min layla: Ø sami:r

By T3 (*yaku:n* Del):

$\Rightarrow$ Ø ?aTwal min layla: Ø sami:r

By T5 (Ag Fronting):

$\Rightarrow$ Ø sami:r Ø ?aTwal min layla:

By T13 and T16:

$\Rightarrow$ Ø sami:run Ø ?aTwalu min layla:

---

[2] This is produces as S_1: 37.

40. S   →   Aux V1   [P N]$_{Erg}$ [P Det N]$_{Ag}$ wa

       →   Aux V1   [P N]$_{Erg}$ [P N]$_{Ag}$

       →   kataba   li   dars   min   ?al   ?awla:d   wa
         ?astaθni: li sami:r min ?ana
           By T1 (Subj P Del):

       ⇒   kataba   li   dars   Ø   ?al   ?awla:d   wa
         ?astaθni: li sami:r Ø ?ana
           By T2 (Obj P Del):

       ⇒   kataba   Ø   dars   Ø   ?al   ?awla:d   wa
         ?astaθni: Ø sami:r Ø ?ana
           By T6 (Erg-Ag Perm):

       ⇒   kataba Ø ?al   ?awla:d Ø   dars wa   ?astaθni: Ø
         ?anna Ø sami:r
           By T14 (N Copying):

       ⇒   kataba   Ø ?al ?awla:d Ø   dars   wa   ?ana:
         ?astaθni: Ø Ø   Ø   sami:r
           By 13 and T16:

       ⇒   kataba   Ø ?al ?awla:du Ø   Ø   wa   ?ana:
         ?astaθni: Ø Ø   Ø   sami:ran
           By T19 (*mubtada? Del):*

       ⇒   kataba   Ø ?al ?awla:du Ø   Ø   wa   Ø
         ?astaθni: Ø Ø   Ø   sami:ran
           By T21 (Special V Tr):

       ⇒   kataba   Ø ?al ?awla:du Ø   Ø   Ø   Ø
         illa   Ø Ø   Ø   sami:ran
           By M-rules

       ⇒   kataba l?awla:du ?illa sami:ran

41. S   →   Aux V1   [P Det N]$_{Erg}$

       →   yaku:n ǰami:l   li   ?al   walad   kita:bat
           By T3 (*yaku:n* Del):

       ⇒   Ø   ǰami:l   li   ?al   walad   kita:bat
           By T18 (Det Tr):

       ⇒   Ø   ǰami:l   li   kita:bat ?al   waladi
           By T1 (Subj P Del):

       ⇒   Ø   ǰami:l   Ø   kita:bat ?al   waladi

By T13 (V1 Agr):

⇒   Ø   ǰami:lat   Ø   kita:bat   ?al   waladi
    By T5 (Erg Fronting):

⇒   Ø   kita:bat   ?al   waladi   Ø   ǰami:lat
    By M-rules

⇒   kita:batu lwaladi ǰami:latun

42. S   →   Aux V1   [P Det NŚ]$_{Erg}$ [P Det N]$_{Inst}$
    → fataha li ?al ba:b ?al ba:b ?ahmar bi ?al mifta:h
       By T2 (Obj P Del):

⇒ fataha Ø   ?al ba:b ?al ba:b   ?ahmar bi ?al mifta:h
       By T33 (Erg-Inst Perm):

⇒ fataha bi ?al mifta:h Ø ?al   ba:b   ?al   ba:b ?ahmar
       By T1 (Subj P Del):

⇒ fataha Ø   ?al mifta:h Ø ?al   ba:b   ?al   ba:b ?ahmar
       By T28 (Adj Tr):

⇒ fataha Ø   ?al mifta:h Ø ?al   ba:b   Ø   ?al   ?ahmar
       By T13 and T16

⇒ fataha Ø   ?al mifta:h Ø ?al   ba:ba Ø   ?al   ?ahmar
       By M-rules:

⇒ fatha lmifta:hu lba:ba l?ahmara

43. S →   Aux V1   [P Det N]$_{Ag}$
    → Emph   maša   min   ?al   walad
       By T1 (Subj P Del):

⇒ Emph   maša   Ø   ?al   walad
       By T13 and T16:

⇒ Emph   maša   Ø   ?al   waladu
       By T23 (Emph Tr):

⇒ maša   Ø   ?al   waladu nafsuhu
       By M-rules:

⇒ maša lwaladu nafsuhu
    Time Aux V1   [P Det N]$_{Ag}$ S

44. S →   → Aux V1 [P N]$_{Ag}$
    → ?amsi maša: min ?al walad maša: min sami:r
       By T1 (Subj P Del):

⇒ ?amsi maša: Ø   ?al walad maša: Ø   sami:r

By T13 and T16:
⇒ ?amsi maša: Ø ?al waladu   maša: Ø sami:run
By T24 (Id. Elem. Del):
⇒ ?amsi maša: Ø ?al waladu Ø   Ø sami:run
By T31 (Time Tr):
⇒ maša: Ø ?al waladu Ø Ø sami:run ?amsi
By M-rules
⇒ maša: lwaladu sami:run ?amsi

45. S → Inter Aux V1   [P N]$_{Erg}$ [P Det N]$_{Erg}$
→ Inter yaku:n Ø li   sami:r   li   ka   ?ism
By T1 (Subj P Del):
⇒ Inter yaku:n Ø Ø   sami:r   Ø ka   ?ism
By T3 (*yaku:n* Del):
⇒ Inter Ø   Ø Ø   sami:r   Ø ka   ?ism
By T18 (Det Tr):
⇒ Inter Ø   Ø Ø   sami:r   Ø ?ism   ka
By T16 (Case Intr.):
⇒ Inter Ø   Ø Ø   sami:run Ø ?ismu ka
By T30 (Inter Tr):
⇒ ma: Ø   Ø Ø Ø   Ø ?ismu ka
By M-rules:
⇒ masmuka

This is an equational sentence, which Fillmore's base cannot account for adequately. It is similar to S25.

46. S → Aux V1   [P Det N S]$_{Erg}$
→ ?inqaTa9a li ?al ħabl ?al ħabl ?ištaraytahu
By T1 (Subj P Del):
⇒ ?inqaTa9a Ø ?al ħabl ?al ħabl ?ištaraytahu
By T22 (Rel. Tr.):
⇒ ?inqaTa9a Ø ?al ħabl ?allaði: ?ištaraytahu
By T13 and T16:
⇒ ?inqaTa9a Ø ?al ħablu ?allaði: ?ištaraytahu
By M-rules:
⇒ ?inqaTa9a lħablu llaði štaraytahu

47. S → Aux V1   [P N]$_{Ag}$ Loc wa S → Aux V1 [P N]$_{Ag}$ Loc
→ maša: min sami:r huna: wa maša: min 9aliyy huna:

---

[3]*sami:run* here is-hum because it means a name and not the boy. That is why it is transformed into *ma:* and not *man.*

By T1 (Subj P Del):

⇒ maša: Ø sami:r huna: wa maša: Ø 9aliyy huna:

By T13 and T16:

⇒ maša: Ø sami:run huna: wa maša: Ø 9aliyyun huna:

By T24 (Id El Tr):

⇒ maša: Ø sami:run huna: wa Ø Ø 9aliyyun huna:

48. S → Inter Aux V1 [P N]$_{Erg}$ [P N]$_{Ag}$

　　→ Inter tusa:9idu li 　　?ana: 　　　min ?anta

　　　　By T1 (Subj P Del):

⇒ Inter tusa:9idu li 　　?ana: 　　Ø ?anta

　　　　By T2 (Obj P Del):

⇒ Inter tusa:9idu Ø 　　?ana: 　　Ø ?anta

　　　　By T14 (N Copying)

⇒ Inter anta 　　tusa9idu Ø 　?ana: Ø Ø

　　　　By T19 (*mubtada?* Del):

⇒ Inter Ø 　　　tusa9idu Ø 　?ana: Ø Ø

　　　　By T30 (Inter Tr):

⇒ ?ala Ø 　　　tusa9idu Ø 　?ana: Ø Ø

　　　　By T13 and T16:

⇒ ?ala Ø 　　　tusa9idu Ø 　i: 　Ø Ø

　　　　By M-rules:

⇒ ?ala: tusa:9iduni:

49. S → Aux V1 [P Det N]$_{Ag}$

　　→ Inter maša: min ?al walad

　　　　By T1 (Subj P Del):

⇒ Inter maša: Ø ?al walad

　　　　By T13 and T16:

⇒ Inter maša: Ø ?al waladu

　　　　By T30 (Inter Tr):

⇒ ?a maša: Ø ?al waladu

　　　　By M-rules:

⇒ ?amaša lwaladu

50. S → ha:ða waladun Ś

This sentence is equational and can be produced in a manner similar to S45 and S25.

　　→ ha:ða waladun sa:fara ?abu:hu

　　　　By T22 (Rel Tr):

⇒ ha:ða waladun sa:fara ?abu:hu

51. S → Aux V1   [P Det N]$_{Erg}$ [P N]$_{Ag}$

      → ?uktub li   ?al dars   min   ?anta
         By T1 (Subj P Del):

      ⇒ ?uktub li   ?al dars   Ø   ?anta
         By T2 (Obj P Del):

      ⇒ ?uktub Ø   ?al dars   Ø   ?anta
         By T14 (N Copying):

      ⇒ ?anta   ?uktub Ø   ?al   darsa Ø   Ø
         By T19 (*mubtada?*
         Del):

      ⇒ Ø   ?uktub Ø   ?al   darsa Ø   Ø
         By M-rules
      ⇒ ?uktub-i-ddarsa

52. S → Condition Aux V1 Erg [P N]$_{Ag}$ +
    S → Aux V1   [P N]$_{Ag}$

      → Condition   tadrusu   Erg min   ?anta +
        tanǰaħu   min   ?anta
         By T7 (Erg Del):

      ⇒ Condition   tadrusu   Ø   min   ?anta +
        tanǰaħu   min   ?anta
         By T1 (Subj P Del):

      ⇒ Condition   tadrusu   Ø   Ø   ?anta +
        tanǰaħu   Ø   ?anta
         By T13 and T16:

      ⇒ Condition   tadrusu   Ø   Ø   ?anta +
        tanǰaħu   Ø   ?anta
         By T14 (N Copying):

  ⇒ Condition ?anta tadrusu Ø   Ø   Ø   +   ?anta
  tanǰaħu   Ø   Ø
         By T19 (*mubtada?* Del)

  ⇒ Condition Ø   tadrusu Ø   Ø   Ø   +   tanǰaħu Ø   Ø
         By T34 (Cond. Tr):

  ⇒ ?in   Ø   tadrus   Ø   Ø   Ø   +   tanǰaħu Ø   Ø

In this chapter, there has been an overall application of the rule of this grammar. In each sentence of the fifty-two sentences of the corpus, there has been a choice from the PS-rules to determine the deep structure of every sentence. Then there has been a choice from the L-rules to supply the deep structure with lexical entities. Then there has been an application of the T-rules to give the deep structure its surface form. Then there has given the final morphophonemic shape of the sentence as it would be allowed by the M-rules, which are not described in this work.

This overall application of the PS-rules, L-rules, and T-rules has shown that this grammar is capable of accounting for the fifty-two sentence corpus. However, it must be admitted that although this grammar can account for this limited corpus and millions of other similar sentences, it may not contain all the probable sentences of the language. Of course, this is a general problem in research: one can always deal with a sample but it is often impractical or impossible to deal with all the population.

CHAPTER EIGHT

CONCLUSIONS AND SUGGESTIONS

The first purpose of this work has been to advise a sample T-grammar of Modern Standard Arabic. This purpose has been achieved by selecting and modifying a suitable PS-model, defending this selection, selecting a corpus, making the L-rules, and finally establishing the necessary T-rules that transform deep structures into surface ones. However, it might be that because of applying Fillmore's model fairly rigorously one may sometimes go counter-intuitively.

The other purpose has been to see how far a base, i.e., Fillmore's, originally devised for English can be used to account for sentences of another language such as Arabic. It has been found that Fillmore's base can efficiently meet the requirements of the deep structure of Arabic sentences, or, more precisely, of those sentences in the corpus. This proves that there is a high degree of university between the deep structures of both Arabic and English.

Comparing the transformations in Arabic and English, it has been found that there is a great deal of similarity between the two languages. Only eight T-rules out of the thirty-four used in Arabic are not used in English: T3, T6, T8, T11, T13, T14, T16, and T32. The other twenty-six T-rules that are used in Arabic are used in English but with a wide variety of degrees of similarity: there is often a partial difference in OBL or OPT, SD, SC, or conditions. This may prove that there is a lot of commonality between Arabic and English in the kinds of transformations used in each.

To conclude, if English and Arabic grammars are compared at the level of surface structures, one finds a limited degree of similarity between them. However, the deep structures, basic functions and kinds of T-rules show a remarkable sameness between the two languages, which argues for universality against the descriptive position which holds that each language is unique and must not be described in terms of other languages.

However, here are some suggestions for further research:

1. Testing the applicability of the same PS-model used in this work i.e., Fillmore's model, to languages other than Arabic – such as French,

Persian, Turkish, Urdu, and Armenian, this may be useful as a further check on the universality of deep structure.

2. Developing the necessary M-rules that operate after the T-rules of Arabic.

3. Comparing Arabic M-rules to English M-rules.

4. Developing the theory of features in the lexical level of Arabic, English, or any other language with some comparative studies.

5. Doing a more elaborate contrastive analysis of Arabic and English based on T-grammar.

6. Developing Aux in Arabic T-grammar and comparing it to Aux in English T-grammar.

7. Looking into the practical application of the T-grammar in teaching English and how the T-theory may affect methods of teaching and learning materials.

PHONEMIC SYMBOLS[1]

/b/	vd	bilabial stop
/t/	vl	dental stop
/d/	vd	dental stop
/T/	vl	dental velarized stop
/D/	vd	dental velarized stop
/k/	vl	velar stop
/q/	vl	uvular stop
/ʔ/	vl	glottal stop
/ǰ/	vd	alveopalatal stop
/f/	vl	labio-dental fricative
/θ/	vl	interdental fricative
/ð/	vd	interdental fricative
/s/	vl	alveolar fricative
/z/	vd	alveolar fricative
/S/	vl	velarized fricative
/Đ/	vd	velarized interdental fricative
/š/	vl	alveopalatal fricative
/x/	vl	velar fricative
/ǥ/	vd	velar fricative
/ħ/	vl	pharyngeal fricative
/9/	vd	pharyngeal fricative
/h/	vl	glottal fricative
/m/	vd	bilabial nasal
/n/	vd	alveolar nasal
/l/	vd	alveolar lateral
/r/	vd	alveolar flap
/w/	vd	bilabial continuant
/y/	vd	palatal continuant
/i/		open high front unrounded vowel
/i:/		open high front unrounded vowel
/a/		close mid central unrounded vowel
/a:/		open low central unrounded vowel
/u/		open high back rounded vowel
/u:/		close high back rounded vowel

---

[1] Raja T. Nasr, *The Structure f Arabic* (Beirut: Librairie Du Liban, 1967), p. 22
However, there have been two minor changes:
(1) z is changed into ǰ to suit the writer's dialect,
(2) – is changed into: to indicate length of vowels.
    In this appendix, vl = voiceless
                vd = voiced
          : = length

NON-PHONEMIC SYMBOLS

+	a boundary of symbols within a string
#	a sentence boundary
→	is re-written (in PS-rules)
⇒	is transformed (in T-rules)
X, Y, Z	cover symbols
( )	optional inclusion of what is inside the parentheses
{ }	one choice within the braces
[ ] [ ]	parallel transformations within the square brackets
Ø	zero (after deletion)
= / —	provided it is followed by
=	means
+	a plus feature in L-rules
—	a minus feature in L-rules
*	intermediate structure
I	first person
II	second person
III	third person
⊃	implies

ABBREVIATIONS[1]

accus. acc	accusative case	OBL	obligatory
Adj	adjective	OPT	optional
Ag	agent	P	preposition
Agr	agreement	Perm	permutation
Aux	auxiliary	Pro	pronoun
Dat	dative	Pros	proposition
Def	definite	PS	phrase structure
Del	deletion	Ref	reflexive
Det	determiner	Rel	relative
DS	deep structure	S	sentence
Erg	ergative	Ś	embedded sentence
Emph	emphatic	SC	structural change
gen	genitive	SD	structural description
gr	grammar	sep	separable
Inst	instrument	sing	singular
Inter	interrogative	Subj	subject
intr	intransitive	T(r)	transformation (al)
L	lexical	Tadj	time adverb
Loc	locative	TG	transformational-generative
M	morphophonemic	tr	transitive
masc	masculine	v, V	verb
nom	nominative	V1	verbal
Obj	object		

---

[1] Arranged according to English alphabet.

GLOSSARY[1]

?a	an interrogative particle	ǰami:l	beautiful (+ masc)
?ab	a father	ǰami:lat	beautiful (− masc)
?aǰmala	beautified	ka	you (accus or gen)
?aħad	someone	kabi:r	large
?aħmar	red	kabura	grew
?a9Ta:	gave	ka:da	was about to
?al	the	ka:na	was
?ala:	an interrogative particle	kataba	wrote
?allaði	relative who or which	ka:tib	writing (present participle)
?amsi	yesterday	kita:b	a book
?aTwal	taller	kita:bat	what is written
?awla:d	more than two boys	qalam	a pen
ba:b	a door	qaTa9a	cut (verb)
bayt	a home	la:	a negative particle
busta:n	a garden; an orchard	lam	a negative particle
bi	instrumental "with"	layla:	Laila (a girl's name)
darasa	studied	ma:	an interrogative particle
dars	a lesson	ma:	a negative particle
Da:ħik	laughing	ma:	something
Daħu:k	cheerful	maktu:bat	written
i:	me, my	maša:	walked
fataħa	opened	mifta:ħ	a key
fi:	in	min	from
ha:ða	this	na:r	fire
hu	his; him	nafsuhu	himself
huna:	here	nahr	a river
huna:ka	there	naǰaħa	succeeded or passed
huwa	he	risa:lat	a letter
ħabl	a rope	sa:fara	travelled
9a:dil	just and fair	sa:9ada	helped
9ala:	on	sa:ra	went
9aliyy	Ali (the name of a person)	ta	you (nom)
9umar	Omar (the name of a person)	Ta:wilat	a table
?iħtira:m	respect (abstract noun)	waqafa	stood up
?inqaTa9a	separated or broke	walad	a boy
?ism	a name	walada:ni	two boys (nom)
?ištara:	bought	waladayni	two boys (accus)
?iyyaka	you (accus)	yaku:n	be (present form)

---

[1] The words are arranged roughly according to English alphabet. The meanings are give according to the context in the corpus.

BIBLIOGRAPHY

ENLISH BOOKS

Allen, Harold B. (ed.). *Readings in Applied English Linguistics.* New York: Appleton-Century-Crofts, 1964.

Bach, Emmon. *An Introduction to Transformational Grammars.* New York: Holt, Rinehart, and Winston, Inc., 1964.

Bach, Emmon and Harms, Robert T. (ed.). *Universals in Linguistic Theory.* London: Holt, Rinehart and Winston, 1968.

Bateson, Mary Catherine. *Arabic Language Handbook.* Washington, D.C.: Center for Applied Linguistics, 1967.

Chafe, Wallace L. *Meaning and the Structure of Language.* Chicago: The university of Chicago Press, 1970.

Chomsky, Noam. *Aspects of the Theory of Syntax.* Cambridge: The M.I.T. Press, 1965.
___. *Syntactic Structures.* The Hague: Mouton and Co., 1957.

Dinneen, F.P. (ed.). *Monograph Series on Languages and Linguistics,* No. 19. Washington, D.C.: Georgetown University Press, 1966.

Gleason, H.A. *An Introduction to Descriptive Linguistics.* New York: Holt, Rinehart, and Winston, 1955.

___. *Linguistics and English Grammar.* New York: Holt, Rinehrt, and Winston, Inc, 1965.

Jacobs, R.A. and Roenbaum, P.S. *English Transformational Grammar.* Waltham: Blaisdell Publishing company, 1968.

Koutsoudas, Andreas. *Writing Transformational Grammars.* New York: McGraw-Hill Book Company, 1966.

Lyons, John. *Introduction to Theoretical Linguistics.* Cambridge: University Press, 1968.

Nasr, Raja T. *The Structure of Arabic.* Beirut: Librairie Du Liban, 1967.

Oldfield, R.C. and Marshall, J.C. (ed.). *Language.* Harmondsworth, England: Penguin Book Ltd., 1968.

Reibel, David A. and Schange, Sanford A. (ed.). *Modern Studies in English.* Englewood Cliffs, New Jersey: Prentice-Hall, Inc., 1969.

Roberts, Paul. *English Syntax.* New York: Harcourt, Brace and World, Inc., 1964.

Thomas, Owen. *Transformational Grammar and the Teacher of English.* New York: Holt, Rinehart, and Winston, Inc., 1965.

Wright, William. (trans. and ed.). *A Grammar of the Arabic Language,* vol. I and II. London: Williams and Norgate, 1862.

Yushmanov, N.V. *The Structure of the Arabic Language.* Trans.: Moshe Perlmann. Washington, D.C.: Center for Applied Linguistics, 1961.

ARABIC BOOKS

Bustani: Butrus. *Mifta:hu AlmiSba:hi fi SSarfi Wannahwi.* Beirut: The American Press, 1895.

Rida, Ali. *?al Mrji9 fi: ?al Lugati ?al 9arabiyyati Nahwiha: waSarfiha:,* Vol. I, II, III. Aleppo: The Syrian Press, 1961.

Shartuni Rasheed. *Maba:di? ?al 9arabiyyati.* Beirut: The Catholic Press, 1955.

ARTICLES

Chomsky, Noam. "Some Methodological Remarks on Generative Grammar" In Allen, Harold B. (ed.). *Readings in Applied English Linguistics.* New York: Appleton-Century-Crofts. 1964. pp. 173-192.

Fillmore, Charles J. "A Proposal Concerning English Prepositions" in Dinneen, F.P. (ed.). *Monograph Series on Languages and Linguistics,* No. 19. Washington, D.C.: Georgetown University Press, 1966, pp. 19-31.

___. "The Case for Case" in Bach, Emmon and Harms, Robert T. (ed.). *Universals in Linguistic Theory.* London: Holt, Rinehart and Winston, 1968, pp. 1-91.

___. "Toward a Modern Theory of Case" in Reibl, David A. and Schane, Sanford A. (ed.). *Modern Studies in English.* Englewood Cliffs, New Jersey: Prentice-Hall, Inc., 1969, pp. 361-375.

Lees, Robert B. "Transformation Grammars and the Fries Framework" in Allen, Harold R.(ed.). *Readings in Applied English Linguistics.* New York: Appleton-Century-Crofts, 1964, pp. 137-146.

Postal, P.M. "Underlying and Superficial Linguistic Structure" in Oldfield, R.C., and Marshall, J.C. (ed.). *Language.* Harmondsworth, England: Penguin Book Ltd., 1968, pp. 179-202.

Thomas, Owen. "Generative Grammar" in Allen, Harold B. (ed.). *Readings in Applied English Linguistics.* New York: Holt, Rinehart, and Winston, Inc., 1964, pp. 405-414.

INDEX

The Author's Books

1. *A Dictionary of Islamic Terms: English-Arabic & Arabic-English*
2. *Simplified English Grammar*
3. *A Dictionary of Education: English-Arabic*
4. *A Dictionary of Theoretical Linguistics: English-Arabic*
5. *A Dictionary of Applied Linguistics: English-Arabic*
6. *Teaching English to Arab Students*
7. *A Workbook for English Teaching Practice*
8. *Programmed TEFL Methodology*
9. *The Teacher of English*
10. *Improve Your English*
11. *A Workbook for English*
12. *Advance Your English*
13. *An Introduction to Linguistics*
14. *Comparative Linguistics: English and Arabic*
15. *A Contrastive Transformational Grammar: English-Arabic*
16. *The Light of Islam*
17. *The Need for Islam*
18. *Traditions of Prophet Muhammad/B1*
19. *Traditions of Prophet Muhammad/B2*
20. *The Truth about Jesus Christ*
21. *Islam and Christianity*
22. *Questions and Answers about Islam*

118

Printed in the United States
By Bookmasters